Religion in Culture

ELEMENTS OF ANTHROPOLOGY
A Series of Introductions

Religion in Culture

Fadwa El Guindi
University of California, Los Angeles

WM. C. BROWN COMPANY PUBLISHERS
Dubuque, Iowa

ANTHROPOLOGY SERIES

Consulting Editors

Frank Johnston
University of Pennsylvania

Henry Selby
Temple University

Library of Congress Catalog Card Number: 76-11977

ISBN 0–697–07549–4

Printed in the United States of America

Contents

	Preface	vii
1	Introduction	1
2	What Is Religion?	5
3	What Does Religion Do?	17
4	Myth and Ritual	25
5	Belief Systems: Concept, Structure, and Meaning	49
	Glossary	65
	Index	69

Preface

I teach kinship and religion, and I always get discouraged by the different attitudes of students toward the two areas. Kinship is serious, intimidating, yet challenging, while religion is a fun course to be taken lightly.

Religion, however, has been systematically studied in anthropology and has developed as a rich area with its own theoretical issues and conceptual sophistication. This book is an attempt to present a challenge to student readers. It tackles core issues and spells out theoretical frameworks, usually considered difficult and thus avoided or superficially brushed over in other synthesizing books. Turner's work in ritual and Lévi-Strauss's work in myth are critically explored in a simplified way with illustrations. In chapter five, I demonstrate a step by step application of structural analysis in myth and ritual of the Zapotec.

Instead of focusing on exotic facts, ethnographic examples are used as illustrations of conceptual points and presented as cases, set off from the body of the text, and consecutively numbered for cross-referencing and for continuity. As often as possible familiar examples from ordinary experience in American life are used.

This book is intended mainly for beginning students, to be used in introductory social/cultural anthropology as a supplement to lectures and other readings, such as those suggested at the end of each chapter. It can also be used in a course on anthropological religion, supplemented by a series of classic articles such as those in Lessa and Vogt's *Reader in Comparative Religion,* and (because of chapters 4 and 5) in a course on structural anthropology. More advanced students can use it to review basic issues and contributions.

My debts are many and my space is limited. However, I would like to acknowledge a special debt to Henry A. Selby, whose "free" creative approach to phenomena has been the major direct influence in the development of my thinking about anthropology. In terms of field work, my whole attitude was shaped by my experience in the Social Research Center, the American University in Cairo. To its Director, Laila El Hamamsy, its Nubian Project Director, Robert A. Fernea, as well as Charles C. Callender and John G. Kennedy, I owe the emphasis on intensive immersion with a people and on detailed collection of data by observation and interviewing. Equally, Harvey Rosenbaum was a force of steady encouragement and insistence on meticulous analysis. The heated stimulating dialogue between us about problems in theoretical linguistics left a permanent impact on what I view to be the appropriate level for a sound analysis. Of course, there is no way to acknowledge the debt I owe the master of contemporary thought on Structure, Claude Lévi-Strauss. His influence in my theoretical orientation is obvious. Roger Keesing's stimulating treatment of anthropological issues and the way "he puts things together" guided my thinking while synthesizing certain issues and problems in parts of this book. Finally, an intangible kind of inspiration that I find difficult to describe comes from my children who refuse to leave me alone to work. And I love them for it.

My students and research assistants contributed in many ways: Joan Bersh, Michael Jacobs, Charles Swagman, and William C. Young. Young deserves special mention since he generously assisted in a number of ways including researching, editing, and criticizing, during writing, typing, and revision of this book. For typing assistance the stenographic pool of the University of California and Tom Kizer from the Department of Anthropology shared the load.

Fadwa El Guindi
University of California, Los Angeles

1 Introduction

DO WE FIGHT OVER RELIGION?

Curiously, if we look at the contemporary "wars" waged in cold or hot form since World War II, we will find that the majority are between countries or groups of different "religions" (Catholic/Protestant, Hindu/Moslem) or "ideologies" (Communist/Capitalist). I include examples of ideologies under the label religion since my view of religion goes beyond dogma that relates only to the supernatural, to a view of religion as a set of notions, concepts, and ideas of a people that serve to order their universe and define its boundaries. A people sharing a culture in its linguistic, economic, political, social, and ecological aspects also share a set of notions drawn from all of these domains about the totality of their system, how its parts are interrelated, and how it works.

This introduction is not an attempt to propose any solution to religious wars or differences based on religion, nor to suggest a causal relationship between the two. But in making a point about conceptual systems, I take the position that such sets of concepts define the ideological boundaries for a group and between groups. Such boundaries put groups in structural positions of potential conflict. The complexity and interrelatedness between territoriality, politics, and propaganda about a people's ideological system activate the differences and reinforce the boundary lines. Ostensibly, it appears as though one group is fighting with the other because one is Christian and the other is Moslem; that is, in theological terms, they may be fighting because of disagreement over whether Jesus was in fact crucified or, as Moslems believe, was saved from crucifixion by God. We all know that such theological matters are not the issue behind these conflicts nor do they constitute a significant part of the total set of notions of a people about their world. But it is these notions that are of interest to us. Where do we look for them? Where do we locate such concepts when we want to study them? The process of how one becomes accepted and categorized in a culture or subculture is a good place to start. For example, let us look at how one is accepted in an American neighborhood.

Case 1: America and Front Lawns.

We rented a house in Manhattan Beach, in southern California. The fact that I am (and look) Egyptian, my husband is (and looks) Jewish American, and that our three-year-old daughter is a green-eyed blonde, unconventional as the combination of all of this may be, did not seem to bring out any overt disapproval on the part of the people already living in the area, called neighbors. But the fact that we did not weed or mow the front lawn upset our neighbors. Our landlady had promised to take care of the lawn but did not, and we could not or would not keep up with it, and before long the front lawn resembled a jungle, violating one of the more basic rules of neighborhood values—keeping one's front lawn well-trimmed all the time.

Why should my lawn bother the people next door? Would Zapotec neighbors in a Zapotec community be as bothered? Doubtful. But in a certain American subculture (middle-class, white, suburban) front lawns are only paid for and cared for by individual families. They really belong to everybody, the neighborhood as community. Everybody decides how lawns should be kept, and there is agreement as to the boundaries of what is acceptable. Violating this rule calls for sanctioning. Neighbors stopped talking to us; the landlady evicted us. We moved out, of course, because we did not like it there anyway; there were no children in the neighborhood to play with our daughter.

Clearly there are different kinds of neighborhoods in America. There are adult neighborhoods, such as the one described in case 1 and there are children's neighborhoods. Front lawns are a good index for sorting out types of American neighborhoods. Obviously a front lawn is very important, otherwise we would not have been evicted. We can use "front lawn" as an index to map a continuum of kinds of neighborhoods based on the degree of trimming and greenness. We can probably find that these correspond to the socioeconomic level of the people responsible for the lawn as well as to their family composition. That is, we could probably tell some things about an American family, such as social and economic status, by looking at their front lawns.

For example, I found out that whenever I am unable to tell whether the grass of a front lawn is real or not until I touch it, then people in that neighborhood are either upper class, with or without children, or upper middle class without children. Such lawns are what I call "crew-cut-trimmed" and very green, no trace of weeds. By contrast, children's neighborhood lawns (middle-class tracts) would be less green, less trimmed, and would hold several-sized tricycles, bicycles, and swings.

Correspondingly, we also find variation in the significant, universe-ordering notions held by people in a neighborhood. Let us look at what happened in a neighborhood different from case 1:

Case 2: You Must Be Pregnant To Live Here.

We bought a house in a middle-class, predominantly Roman Catholic tract full of children of all ages in Redondo Beach, in southern California. Four months had passed, and children avoided playing with our daughter. It could not have been our lawn this time since we managed to maintain it at least as well as some of the minimally maintained lawns in the same neighborhood.

It was crucial for us to succeed in this community because our child needed playmates. So I decided to move out to the mothers of those children and "establish rapport" just as we do as anthropologists in the field. The conversations focused on my career and profession. The others were curious about what work I do, how I managed the three roles of professional, wife, and mother. They wanted to know who took care of my four-year-old daughter when I was at work.

I explained that the real problem I have to face will be when the new baby arrived. I was pregnant. "Baby" or "pregnant" must have been the magic word. They had not been aware that I was pregnant. It did not matter what I said afterwards; being Egyptian, being "Moslem," married to a "Jew," nothing mattered.

This knowledge became public and passed around the neighborhood quite fast. I could not keep up with the doorbell ringing by children asking to play with my daughter Magda. The change was too sudden to be coincidental.

Of course establishing rapport in a middle-class American tract is in many ways no different from working toward being accepted in a Zapotec community near Oaxaca City in Mexico.

Case 3: We All Have the Same Blood.

Not being the more familiar "gringa" anthropologist, my presence in the Zapotec community in 1967 posed some difficulty for the natives since they could not readily draw upon the usual resources available to them for categorizing outsiders, who are American anthropologists. Approximately two or three weeks had passed after my arrival without any overt gesture of acceptance.

Then a local man came to me and initiated the following conversation:

"So, you are Egyptian you say?"

"Yes."

"We still use the plow that Egyptians had invented."

"Yes."

"You are Arab then?"

"Yes."

"Of course the Arabs ruled the Spaniards for a long time. . ."

"Yes."

". . . and the Spaniards ruled us. . ."

(I began to be nervous. Would he then accuse me of indirect imperialism?) He stretched out his arm and vigorously shook my hands saying,

"We have the same blood!"

This is a kinship statement. I became categorized through one of the most valuable categorizing channels for the Zapotec: kinshipping. And that was just the beginning. Despite their full awareness that my husband and I are not Roman Catholics, and more specifically that I am "Moslem" and my husband is "Jewish" we were requested to become godparents and coparents, thus joining the Zapotec Roman Catholic network of fictive kinship relationships.

Though in each case the details are unique, the three cases involve beliefs about how the universe is ordered and notions about the boundaries of what is acceptable. To be accepted in a cultural group a newcomer cannot violate this "order." If so, the newcomer is rejected. If not, the natives will search for means from domains that are meaningful within their own system to categorize the newcomer and thus allow her or him to "enter the community."

As we have seen in all three ethnographic cases, the categories of people involved were of different religions. Yet in all three cases the theological differences were ignored. They all involve beliefs and values that are an important part of their system. The ideas and notions about their orderly universe can be drawn from different domains in their culture or subculture. In case 1 the natives of that neighborhood cannot allow a jungle of weeds in their spatial domain. It also tells them something about ours that made us not worthy of approval. In case 2 since I am out working in the public domain (that is, male domain) it should also follow that I probably space my children "immorally" and am possibly for abortion and probably am neglecting my one girl, etc. . . . Being pregnant makes me more "human" in the sense of "normal." It denies all these other aspects. In case 3 I was very careful to "establish rapport" in the proper manner. I became accepted. So all they had to do is to categorize me within their system.

But how does all this relate to religion, which is what this book is supposed to be about? My examples point toward a view of religion that is not merely hymns and incense, catechisms and sermons, but religion as lived in specific communities and as the way people think of the world around them. It is religion *in* culture, integrating the community, the natural world, and thought.

For Further Reading

Berger, Peter L., and Luckmann, Thomas. *The Social Construction of Reality*. Garden City,

New York: Doubleday & Co., 1967. A philosophical and empirical investigation of the relation between society and knowledge. The influence of social "objects" (such as class, roles, social rules) on the individual's mind and his contribution toward constructing these objects are explored. What every student of theory in the social sciences should know.

2 What Is Religion?

THE ANTHROPOLOGICAL VIEW OF RELIGION

The nature of religion is a problem which has occupied philosophers, historians, theologians, and other scholars in different parts of the world for centuries. In general, scholarship work on religion prior to the 19th century was characterized by four features. First, the focus was on world religions, e.g., Islam, Christianity, Judaism; other forms of religion, even when known, were not considered. Second, studies on religion were ethnocentric. That is, any statements made about religion were from the point of view of the scholar's own world religion (evaluations of premises and principles of any religion were based on the moral, philosophical, and logical standards of the scholar's religion). Third, the questions addressed and arguments made were philosophical and speculative rather than empirical. Fourth, there was a concern with absolute truth.

The first sustained efforts to understand and interpret the phenomenon of religion in the Western tradition began with works of 19th century British and French scholars. This period was marked by technological, social, and intellectual change as well as considerable travel. Explorers, missionaries, soldiers, and scholars were going to parts of the world that were previously untouched, collecting information and documenting customs and ways of life of non-Western peoples. As a result we find that knowledge about non-Western ways was accumulating.

Another prominent feature of that period was the impact of the theory of evolution on the biological and social sciences. Evolutionary concepts were dominant. Just as biologists were interested in determining the origin, development, and differentiation of organisms, anthropologists were interested in determining the origin, development, and differentiation of cultures.

The third prominent feature of that period was the beginning of man's awareness of his antiquity. We had not realized before how "old" we are as a species. The discovery of Paleolithic tools and the different physical types of ancient man made us realize that our history was much longer than was previously believed.

These findings: the discovery of Paleolithic Man, the development of the theory of evolution, and the discovery of peoples previously unknown, influenced 19th century scholarship in every way. Moreover, such discoveries were in conflict with the teachings of the Bible. Much of this new knowledge was not accounted for in the Bible and indicated a need to reevaluate ideas that had previously been considered unquestionable. This resulted in a long struggle between scholarship and the Church.

The same questions about the nature of man and society that were raised by the social philosophers before the 19th century continued to be the focus of inquiry. There was a change, however, in the way these issues were investigated. One crucial change was the shift toward empiricism. Anthropologists looked for empirical facts both in secondary sources (those accounts from travelers and missionaries) and through their own direct field research.

It is also important to consider the specific effect that the notion of evolution had on anthropological studies. Scholars sought to fit specific facts to evolutionary schemes in an attempt to determine the developmental sequence of cultural phenomena. However, anthropologists of that period were very much influenced by the socioreligious standards of their time. Being Victorian meant reaching the peak of social evolutionary development. Being Christian meant reaching the peak of religious evolutionary development. All others belonged to the category "prelogical savage." In other words, the prevalent assumption was that phenomena developed from a worse state to a better one. The worse state is the savage, the better one is the Victorian. This was the new form of ethnocentrism.

The study of religion followed that same pattern. Cross-cultural facts about religion were fit into developmental schemes. All religions were thought to represent evolutionary stages between polar opposites. Religion was seen within a framework of progressive development as passing through linear stages from savagery to civilization. All evolutionary schemes formulated at that time to account for religion contained the concept of progress.

Anthropologists addressed themselves to such basic questions as: How did religion begin? What form or forms did it take? How did it develop? It was believed that the earliest form of religion could be determined by studying contemporary "primitive" religions. The various simple forms of religion could then be located on an evolutionary scale to find the accurate history of all religion, leading of course to Christianity.

Twentieth-century scholarship moved away from the concept of evolution as a process of improvement and progress. The anthropological study of religion accordingly changed its emphasis. Throughout most of this century social scientists have been predominantly concerned with comparative studies, that is, studies focusing on specific cultures and comparing these cultures with each other. Studies of origin and development lost their place in anthropology. Most current studies reject the idea of progress and, except for one adaptational school of thought, lean toward nonevolutionary approaches.

THE NATURE OF RELIGION

Questioning the relationship between religion and society is not new. There was interest in it from ancient Greek times to the present day. But one of the first "scientific" efforts to examine empirically that relationship was that of the 14th-century Arab scholar Ibn Khaldun (1332-1406). He investigated the question of society as a basis for religion within the general context of the "science of culture," which he undertook to formulate.

Ibn Khaldun's science of culture was born because he needed to understand things that seemed obscure. He was intrigued by various problems and questions that raised themselves as part of the history of Western Islam (North Africa) at the time. He was dissatisfied with purely historical or philosophical treatments of the issues and basically addressed himself to man and his relationship to society. Therefore he proceeded to isolate certain principles that formed the foundation of a new science: the science of culture.

Ibn Khaldun's theory is an exception to pre-19th-century scholarship. Many of his interesting ideas have reappeared in same or similar form long after his death, in 19th-century and early 20th-century anthropological contributions. As a Moslem he utilized principles from Islam as a point of departure in his universal theory on culture. His study is empirical; it is based on his own observations and examination of various Arab and Moslem societies and groups as well as drawing on facts from secondary sources.

Solidarity and Religion

Ibn Khaldun starts his inquiry by isolating certain principles. The first of these principles is that society is necessary; the second is that man and society are internally (through man's physical constitution) and externally related to the physical environment; and the third is that man and society are related (through man's rational faculty) to the spiritual world, the world beyond perceptible natural beings.

The most important distinction made by Ibn Khaldun relevant to our discussion of religion as well as to general anthropological theory is the distinction between primitive culture (*'umrān badawi*) and civilized culture (*'umrān ḥaḍari*). Primitive culture is defined primarily as a way of life that concentrates on the cultivation of land and raising domesticated animals, whether the people are settled or nomadic. It is a simple way of life geared toward the satisfaction of the most simple and necessary needs.

Communities are small and self-supporting; food is simple and requires little processing; clothes are made of animal skins or handwoven materials; and shelter is in the form of caves, tents, or simple huts. None but the most necessary tools and arts are present. There are no cities or public works, and no market economy or taxation. Literacy is sparse, the arts are based on fragmentary and insufficient experience, and there is no body of organized rational knowledge.

This simplicity in economic, political, and social organization is accompanied by a simple form of *'aṣabiyya*—social solidarity. Common ancestry, common interests, and common experiences of life and death reinforce each other in developing the feeling of solidarity.

However, primitive culture does not remain static. Small groups increase in size, political structure becomes more complex, and primitive culture becomes influenced by the desire for power, riches, and leisure, thus developing and changing toward civilization.

For that transformation to take place a strong force is created to enhance and reinforce the already existing solidarity. This force is religion. Religion, according to Ibn Khaldun, is a social phenomenon established through solidarity and usually born among groups with strong solidarity. Once a religion is adopted and supported by such a group, it becomes a highly effective force. It creates a new loyalty: absolute belief in divine law and obedience to the religious leader.[1]

This relationship between religion and societal solidarity is best seen as dialectical. No attempt is made to define religion. It is clear, however, that Ibn Khaldun's concept of religion was not limited to world religions of monotheistic deities and associated prophecy. He observed that the peoples who have a divinely revealed book and who follow prophets (Islam, Christianity, Judaism) are small in number in comparison with peoples who have other forms of religion,

1. Muhsin Mahdi, *Ibn Khaldun's Philosophy of History* (Chicago: University of Chicago Press, 1971), pp. 159-204.

and that nonmonotheistic societies develop into big civilizations as well.[2]

These simple societies characterized by simplicity in the various aspects of social organization interested anthropologists of the 19th century so much so that they became the focus of their study.

Regarding the domain of religion, questions like whether religion concerns one supreme deity or several deities, whether it involves a belief or also associated action and ritual, or whether it focuses on supernatural beings or natural forces, began as vital issues in 19th-century anthropology and continue to be discussed until the present day. A growing trend toward objectivity and the scientific method raised these issues. Several attempts were made to find a simple definition delineating phenomena that are "religious" from those that are not.

Belief in the Supernatural

Edward B. Tylor (1832-1917) was the first to offer a definition of religion. He defined it as "the belief in spiritual beings," or animism. This belief both underlies all religions in the world and represents the earliest form of religion. His orientation is that religion is a rational attempt on the part of humans to interpret mysterious phenomena. One important aspect of Tylor's theory of animism is the concept of soul. It is man's theory about the mysterious phenomena of death, sleeping, and dreaming, three of the many questions that preoccupied primitive people.

Tylor's theory goes this way. Man had a *phantom,* a *life,* and a *material body.* Life enabled the body to be a sentient being, and the phantom was the body's image, or second self. The combination of life and phantom formed the concept of soul which could detach itself from the body and wander about, appearing in dreams.[3]

I became aware of how the Zapotec are preoccupied with similar questions when my key female informant talked about her dreams: "The souls wander around when one is sleeping, otherwise how can people who are actually living far away appear in one's dreams?"

Case 4: Dreams.

The Zapotec believe that persons have three components: body, soul, and animal. A person's soul leaves the body temporarily and wanders around. This happens when a person is asleep and dreaming. The souls get together; that is how one person can dream of another who is physically far away from him. The soul can be visible in the form of a white moth. In death the soul permanently leaves the body. A black moth is a sure sign that someone has just died.

The story goes that there was once a priest who had a cat. This cat slept with him in bed. One morning the priest slept late and neighbors knocked on his door to wake him up. They knocked and knocked because he was late for church. But he did not wake up and his neighbors figured that the cat must have eaten his wandering soul. It is dangerous to let cats sleep near people because they eat moths. They searched for the cat, and when they found her, they cut her stomach open, and sure enough a moth came flying out. When they went back to the priest's room they found that he was up.

But since the dead as well as the living appear in dreams, Tylor says, it is believed that the soul continues to live after death. The Zapotec would certainly agree with this notion. In fact the Zapotec believe that their dead return once a year to visit their families during the All Saints period.

2. Ibn Khaldun, *The Muqaddimah: An Introduction to History,* 2nd ed. (Princeton: Princeton University Press, 1967), p. 93.

3. Edward B. Tylor, "Animism," in *Reader in Comparative Religion,* eds. W. A. Lessa and E. Z. Vogt (New York: Harper & Row, 1972), pp. 9-19.

In Zapotec native theory, however, the immortality of the soul is not their explanation for the appearance of the dead in dreams.

Case 5: The Dead Take the Food.

The Zapotec dead come on All Saints (*Todos Santos*) every year to visit their families. All Saints involves three days of elaborate activities and preparation of food to receive the dead visitors. Every household competes in decorating its altar with as much food, drink, fruits, nuts, flowers, candles, and incense as they can borrow or afford to buy. These items are for the dead visitors who come to the altar and "take" the food, drink, and candles.

The people know that the dead come because there are several signs of arrival: objects moving on the altar or falling from the altar to the floor, insects crawling on the food, or moths flying around the altar. These are signs that the dead have come. They also know that the dead eat the food because foods are found later stripped of odor and flavor. The dead take them.

Animatism: Belief in Natural Force

As knowledge about primitive religion increased, scholars questioned the universality of animism as the basis of all religions. Robert R. Marett (1866-1943) postulated that there existed a preanimistic stage of religion where primitive man simply recognized the power existing in nature and certain objects. He claimed that the concept of *mana* is universal and thus basic to his theory of animatism.

His theory is based on the belief that powers (*mana*) exist in nature or in objects and create in humans religious feelings of awe, fear, wonder, respect, and admiration. *Mana* is a label derived from Polynesia which refers to an impersonal force, not unlike electricity in industrial society. *Mana* can be compared with electricity because both are considered forces rather than properties, behaviors, or beliefs, and both can be controlled by man and used for good or bad. Both could be particularly bad when out of control.

Marett's notion was that primitive man did not conceive of any natural order. Primitive man, according to Marett, could not distinguish between the "natural" and the "supernatural." Even though he could distinguish between the "living" and the "dead," he did consider certain things, such as stones for example, as "animate", i.e., as having life, hence, the theory of animatism.[4]

SACRED AND PROFANE

Another attempt at finding the common denominator for all religions was made by Émile Durkheim (1858-1917). He defined religion as: "a unified system of beliefs and practices relative to sacred things, that is to say, things set apart and forbidden—beliefs and practices which unite into one single moral community called a Church, all those who adhere to them."[5] This definition contains Durkheim's basic position and arguments, which perhaps become clearer if we break the definition into major segments and discuss each segment separately.

According to Durkheim, religion is "a unified system of belief and practices. . . ." This means that religion is best seen as a system of interrelated parts. The two fundamental categories within that system are beliefs and rites. Beliefs, to Durkheim, are states of opinion translated in tangible form through symbolic representations; rites are determined modes of action. By asserting that religion is both beliefs and rites, Durk-

4. R. R. Marett, *The Threshold of Religion,* 2nd ed. (London: Methuen & Co., 1914), pp. 14, 18, 118.

5. Emile Durkheim, *The Elementary Forms of the Religious Life,* trans. J. W. Swain (New York: Collier Books, 1961), p. 62.

heim has taken a position against previous assertions, particularly those of Tylor and Marett, that religion is only belief.

The two areas of belief (myth) and rites (ritual) remain important in the anthropological study of religion and are systematically studied. At one point their interrelationship was a live issue in 19th-century theory, and it was recently revived again in the work of Claude Lévi-Strauss. This will be explored in more detail in chapter 4.

Religion is ". . . . relative to sacred things. . . ." In other words, religion presupposes a distinction, a classification of all things, real and ideal, into sacred and profane. Sacred are those things "set apart and forbidden," things dangerous and holy. All things which are not sacred are profane. The profane consists of ordinary, everyday things not given any special importance by society. There is nothing mysterious nor unexplainable about either domain.

Tylor had argued earlier that religion arises when man confronts his environment and is faced with mysterious, obscure phenomena that he cannot explain. In his rational attempt to explain such mysteries primitive man develops animistic beliefs about spirit beings.

Contrary to Tylor's notion, Durkheim asserts sacred things can be found in regularly occurring sociological phenomena. Nothing is unknowable to man, primitive or modern, because everything is accessible to the explanatory capacity of humans. Every event is potentially amenable to absorption in man's conceptual order.

Whereas to Tylor religion was belief in supernatural beings and to Marett it was belief in natural forces, Durkheim's religion is the sacred sphere of life found in society. He bases his view on the empirical fact that there are religions in the world, like Buddhism, that do not espouse belief in the supernatural nor in the natural.

Even though Durkheim sets up this conceptual distinction between the domain of sacred and the domain of profane as a useful universal dichotomy, he takes the relativistic position that societies differ in the things that they set apart and perceive as sacred.

Case 6: Flags and Rivers: Sometimes Sacred, Sometimes Not.

Let us consider, for example, the flag in American culture. It is a sacred symbol. Certain behaviors, such as spitting on it, tearing it, flying it upside down, or, as has been happening recently since the late 1960s, wearing it as clothing (to express cynicism about Americanity!) are not tolerated, are considered disrespectful, and are disapproved of.

"Flag," however, is meaningless in Nubia. When I was doing field research in Nubia during 1962 and 1963 I observed that flags are used for decoration during their local celebrations. As such it never mattered to the Nubians of Dahmit which flag was flying. Obsolete Turkish flags alongside obsolete (royal) Egyptian flags decorated the area where the ritual was celebrated. No holy attitude is associated with flags for the Nubians nor are flags very important. In fact, most of those used were torn and worn out, easily replaceable by plain rags.

The contrary is true with "river." Rivers in American culture are profane in Durkheimian language. No sacredness or special meaning is given to them in the United States. In Nubia and Egypt, on the other hand, the river Nile has been considered sacred throughout Egyptian and Nubian history, and remains actively so in the rural and Nubian parts of Egypt. The belief that there are superhuman beings in the river, sacrificial offerings and propitiations, along with elaborate ritual directly related to the Nile, are examples of the importance a culture gives to "ordinary things," thus making them sacred.

Thus, in Durkheim's words, the real characteristic of religious phenomena is that they always presuppose a bipartite division of the known and knowable universe into two all-embracing but radically exclusive categories. The heterogeneity of the two worlds is so complete (and here the influence of evolutionary thinking on Durkheim's theory shows) that in developed religions it leads to the establishment of the concept that sacred and profane spheres are hostile to each other, the monastery posed against the world.[6]

Religions ". . . unite all those who adhere to them. . . . The Durkheimian position is that religion is a system which expresses and maintains the values and sentiments of society in its collective consciousness through group activity in ritual and ceremony. People are social beings, members of the society in which they were born and raised. There is no thought uninfluenced by a person's society.

Like Ibn Khaldun, Durkheim asserts that religion is not in any way a matter of individual originality or eccentricity; it is a social phenomenon. Certainly new religions come into existence, but these are products of their society rather than individual innovations.

Again as in Ibn Khaldun's theory of culture and solidarity, the notion of community is fundamental. Religion is preeminently a collective phenomenon. All great social institutions have had their origin in religion. Religion has given birth to all that is essential in society, and the idea of society is the soul of religion.

Whereas for Tylor what is religious is supernatural, for Durkheim (as for Ibn Khaldun) what is religious is sociological; it is society that develops symbols to express and maintain what is collectively "sacred." Religious representations are collective ones that express collective realities; rites are designed to excite, maintain, or recreate certain mental states in human groups.

Religions unite ". . . into one single moral community called a Church." As soon as humans became members of a society they must have regulated their behavior toward one another to "live together." Durkheim argues that religion is concerned with this regulation of behavior.

Each society sets up rules, regulations, and symbols of important things. The learning and internalization of these rules and symbols is a major part of the socialization of each person. The rules and symbols themselves may seem trivial, but they represent the vital issue of conformity to the social system.

Religion, in that framework, is a major form of social control. The socialized individual feels an element of danger or feels wrong and guilty if he does not behave in a fashion acceptable to his social group or if he violates the rules of his social system. It is tempting to look at traffic rules in American society as an example. Such rules are rigid, well-defined, and considered extremely important. A properly socialized American will feel wrong or even guilty driving through a red light, even under "safe" conditions, at late night hours, and when it is certain that there are no traffic officers in sight. Traffic violation is so "un-American" that it is included as a crime along with adultery, polygamy, belief in communism, and other issues in the naturalization forms for aliens. That is, these are items of considerable importance, which express the basic notion of being an "ideal American citizen." These are "sacred things" in American culture.

A religion, according to Durkheim, is a totality of beliefs and corresponding rites constituted from a certain number of sacred things. These are in a relationship of coordination or subordination with each other in

6. Ibid., pp. 54, 55, 350.

such a fashion as to form a system having a certain unity.[7]

Church is used in the broad sense of moral community. It involves the notion of collectivity and hence is a basic aspect of religion. In fact, church is used by Durkheim to distinguish between religion and magic. There is no church of magic.

Religious life has its foundation in groups. A society feels itself united by the commonality of its beliefs; members become united by the fact that they think in the same way regarding the sacred world and translate these common ideas into common practice which comprises what is termed a church. Magic, on the other hand, does not bind together its adherents. Between the magician and his patrons there are only temporary ties.[8]

Clearly, whether he is discussing religion or he is distinguishing between religion and magic, Durkheim is really talking about society.

RELIGION, MAGIC, SCIENCE

Sir James Frazer (1854-1941) and Bronislaw Malinowski (1884-1942) tell us that there is a difference between religion and magic, and that there is a significant relationship between magic and science. By claiming that religion and magic are different, Frazer and Malinowski were saying that these two labels represent two actual, distinguishable classes of actions and beliefs. They argue that religion and magic have similarities in that both are supernatural, both are rich in symbolism, and both are characterized by elaborate ritual. Yet they are basically quite different.

Religion is supplicative; by ritual it conciliates superhuman powers to request favors. Magic is manipulative; it acts ritually on superhuman powers to automatically make use of them. It is a formula or set of formulas. It is not a force as is *mana*.

Frazer examined magic in detail. According to his analysis, there are two major principles involved in the operation of magic: the law of similarity, and the law of contagion or contact. The law of similarity is the principle "like produces like," or that an effect resembles its cause.

The law of contagion or contact is the principle that things, once in contact with each other, continue to act on each other at a distance after the physical contact has been severed. The first principle in action means that the practitioner believes that he can produce any effect he desires merely by imitating it; the second, that whatever he does to a material object will affect in the same way the person with whom the object was once in contact, whether it formed a part of his body or not.

Charms based on the law of similarity are called "homeopathic" or "imitative magic." Charms based on the law of contact or contagion may be called "contagious magic." Both are "sympathetic magic." Frazer diagrams the branches of magic according to the laws of thought which underlie them as follows:

FIGURE 2.1
FRAZER'S CLASSIFICATION OF MAGIC

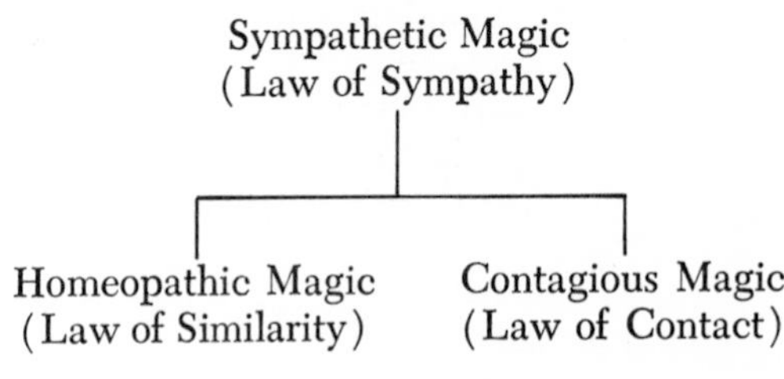

Frazer asserts that magic is primitive man's attempt at science, but that it is only a pseudoscience. He maintains that the logic of the magician was an erroneous applica-

7. Ibid., pp. 56, 478.
8. Ibid., p. 60.

tion of the two laws of similarity and contact. Homeopathic magic is founded on the association of ideas by similarity; contagious magic is founded on the association of ideas by contiguity.

Homeopathic magic commits the mistake of assuming that things that resemble each other are the same; contagious magic commits the mistake of assuming that things which have once been in contact with each other are always in contact. But in practice the two branches are often combined.[9]

Only "Civilized" Man Thinks Well?

Frazer argued that the primitive magician knows magic only in terms of its practical side; he never analyzes the mental processes on which his practice is based, never reflects on the abstract principles involved in his actions. In short, magic to him is always an art, never a science; the very idea of science is lacking in his undeveloped mind.

It is important to see Frazer in context. He is a product of 19th-century ethnocentric evolutionary thinking. His notion is that religion should be distinguished from magic. Magic is closer to science. But since "primitive" people have undeveloped minds they use magic. As they develop into "civilized" people they begin to employ science. Here, magic and science are the polar opposites in the developmental scheme.

Frazer's claims about "savage thought" are strong and unsupported. When the tradition of "fieldwork" began with Malinowski, a whole orientation followed where anthropologists rejected "armchair" claims and speculations based on secondary sources, immersing themselves instead among tribal peoples and studying their ways of life in detail. Malinowski studied the Trobriand Islanders and examined their behavior and social system. Based on his observations and analysis he rejected Frazerian ideas about the undeveloped mind of primitives. He also questioned assertions made by French scholar Lévy-Bruhl (1857-1939) that primitive man is hopelessly immersed in a mystical frame of mind, devoid of the power of abstraction, and prelogical in his outlook on the universe.[10]

Malinowski felt that magic had been misunderstood. He said that the Trobrianders use both magic and science, but that we need to understand the relationship between the two. His firsthand experience with the Trobrianders shows that they possess a rich store of empirical and rational knowledge about their environment and how to use it. They are fully aware of their resources and know how to manipulate them to their advantage. Constrained by the limits of Neolithic technology, how could "primitive" man carve out a niche and exploit it as well as he has? He must necessarily be a "scientist."

Trobrianders, like all people, use their technology, whatever its level, with great skill and know-how, to ensure abundant life from their environment. They "depend on their agricultural success, which in turn depends on an extensive knowledge of soil conditions, plant types, mutual relationships between the two, and hard, accurate work."[11] Yet, despite all the effort and skill in gardening, in fighting, in love, or in the *kula,* sometimes there are failures. Their skill, knowledge, and hard work does not necessarily ensure success in all aspects of Trobriand life. Crops do fail, *kula* exchanges become blocked, canoes are destroyed, lovers are disappointed, etc.

9. James G. Frazer, "Sympathetic Magic," in *Reader in Comparative Religion,* pp. 415-430.

10. Lucien Lévy-Bruhl, *The "Soul" of the Primitive,* trans. L. A. Clare (Chicago: Henry Regnery Co., 1971), pp. 16-17, 154-155.

11. Bronislaw Malinowski, "The Role of Magic and Religion," in *Reader in Comparative Religion,* p. 64-65.

So "the native knows full well that there are natural conditions and causes, and by his observations he knows physical and mental effort can control them. But experience teaches him that despite all his efforts, there are agencies and forces which one year bestow tremendous fertility, and in another year bring ill-luck. To control these influences and these *only* he employs magic."[12] Magic, according to Malinowski, is a body of purely practical acts, performed as a means to an end. By knowing the magical spell, a man controls a form of power conferred on his people by the ancestors who emerged from beneath the earth. Magic is regarded as indispensable to the welfare of the gardens, and at every step of communal gardening the magician must perform magical rites—use of words which invoke, state, or command the desired end—with reference to mythological elements.[13] So the magic is to ensure success and is in addition to human skill.

Does this mean that the Trobrianders are naive in dealing with the world? Is there a sharp difference between the prelogical thinking of the native and the sophistication of scientists? Where and how is a boundary drawn between magic and primitive "science"?

Malinowski tells us that the Trobrianders keep magic conceptually apart from empirical knowledge. Magic "serves to bridge over the dangerous gaps in every important pursuit or critical situation. The function of magic is to ritualize man's optimism, to enhance his faith in the victory of hope over fear."[14]

More recent studies, however, and certainly my own investigation of the Zapotec, suggest that the differentiation between a people's magic and their science as two conceptual categories is more a function of the scholar's taxonomic view of the native's world rather than reflecting empirical reality. I am unable to draw the line between Zapotec behavior that is magical and that which is scientific. Systems are more complicated than that, and certainly more subtly integrated.

But to go back to the effect of magic. What if after all the combined effort, scientific and magical, magic does not work? That is, what if crops do fail, lovers do separate, villages become defeated, etc.? If we look at the beliefs of any people we will find a fund of concepts stored and available for them to draw on whenever there is need for explanation. Let us take the Egyptian Nubians as an example.

Case 7: The "Evil Eye" and Mushahra.

Two important concepts that the Nubians believe in are the "evil eye" and *mushahra*. Belief in the evil eye is widespread in Nubia, as in the entire Middle East. Prosperity, good fortune, beauty, and any other attribute that may draw attention and admiration were held to expose one to the envy of others and to the evil eye. Its effects range from illness to misfortune. For example, one day as we were returning from an exhausting trip to a saint's celebration in a neighboring district, I became ill. The villagers insisted that it is my ability to speak and sing in Mettokki which drew praise from other women that brought envy and "evil eye." Many other ordinary misfortunes were consistently explained in terms of "evil eye."

Mushahra is a term derived from the Arabic *shahr* (month) and means potential threat or danger. It is generally introduced through carelessness rather than malice. It requires direct contact with an agent. The most common agent was gold jewelry. Other agents are eggplant

12. Ibid., p. 66.
13. Ibid., p. 67.
14. Bronislaw Malinowski, *Magic, Science and Religion* (Garden City, New York: Doubleday & Co., 1954), p. 90.

and uncooked meat, experiences such as crossing the Nile, a man who had just shaved or cut his hair, any person, of either sex, who did not bathe ritually after intercourse, anyone who had attended a funeral, seen a corpse or a burial procession, or come from giving condolences for death, those who were recently themselves vulnerable to mushahra, women who were recently delivered or had weaned a child, and children who had been circumcised or excised.[15]

In other words, we find that a system of beliefs is rich in concepts that can serve as explanatory devices for the natives. "Evil eye" or *mushahra* are not directly controlled by anybody and are difficult to avoid by their very nature. If all science and magic fails it must be then "evil eye" or *mushahra.*

More recently, Lévi-Strauss in his *Savage Mind,* revives the issue of the claimed dichotomy between "primitive" thought and "civilized" thought. For both, he argues, the universe is an object of thought. He feels that, instead of contrasting magic and science, as Frazer and Malinowski did, it is better to compare them as two parallel modes of acquiring knowledge. He rejected Frazer's notion of pseudoscience and Malinowski's notion of spurious science. "Our view is that the kind of logic in mythical thought is as rigorous as that of modern science, and that the difference lies, not in the quality of the intellectual process, but in the nature of the things to which it is applied." He uses an example from the field of technology:

"What makes a steel ax superior to a stone ax is not that the first one is better made than the second. They are equally well made, but steel is quite different from stone. In the same way we may be able to show that the same logical processes operate in myth as in science, and that man has always been thinking equally well; the improvement lies, not in an alleged progress of man's mind, but in the discovery of new areas to which it may apply . . . its powers. . . ."[16]

For Further Reading

Lévi-Strauss, Claude. *The Savage Mind.* Chicago: University of Chicago Press, 1966. A fascinating, though complex, description of the logical problems and schemes that people in nonliterate societies apply their energies to. The book is both an illustration of the thought of primitive peoples and Levi-Strauss's own thinking. Read slowly but with determination; the book will have a lasting effect on your ideas about primitive people, and so is well worth the effort of reading it. But in general do become too involved with details.

Mahdi, Muhsin. *Ibn Khaldun's Philosophy of History.* Chicago: University of Chicago Press, 1971. A discussion of the methods and conclusions of the first social scientist. Especially recommended for those interested in the history of ideas. Provides exposure to a non-Western approach to social science.

Malinowski, Bronislaw. *Coral Gardens and Their Magic.* 2 vols. London: George Allen & Unwin, 1935. A classic work illustrating Malinowski's distinction between religion and magic, and the "function" of both of these in satisfying man's needs. Skim to get a feel for his approach. Details are fun to read.

Bibliography

Callender, Charles and El Guindi, Fadwa. 1971. *Life-Crisis Rituals among the Kenuz.* Cleveland: Press of Case Western Reserve University.

Durkheim, Émile. 1961. *The Elementary Forms of the Religious Life.* Translated by J. W. Swain. New York: Collier Books.

15. Charles Callender and Fadwa El Guindi, *Life-Crisis Rituals among the Kenuz,* no. 3 (Cleveland, Ohio: Press of Case Western Reserve University, 1971), pp. 11-15.

16. Claude Lévi-Strauss, "The Structural Study of Myth," in *Structural Anthropology* (New York: Basic Books, 1963), p. 230.

Frazer, James G. 1972. "Sympathetic Magic." In *Reader in Comparative Religion.* Edited by W. A. Lessa and E. Z. Vogt. New York: Harper & Row.

Ibn Khaldun. 1967. *The Muqaddimah: An Introduction to History.* Translated by Franz Rosenthal. Princeton, New Jersey: Princeton University Press.

Lévi-Strauss, Claude. 1963. *Structural Anthropology.* New York: Basic Books.

Malinowski, Bronislaw. 1954. *Magic, Science and Religion.* Garden City, New York: Doubleday & Co.

Marett, R. R. 1914. *The Threshold of Religion.* London: Metheun & Co.

Tylor, Edward B. 1972. "Animism." In *Reader in Comparative Religion.* Edited by W. A. Lessa and E. Z. Vogt. New York: Harper & Row.

3 What Does Religion Do?

As we have seen, early theorists asked the questions, "What is religion?" and "What is its origin?" Then they tried to describe the varieties of religious customs by labeling and pigeonholing the various "types" of religions. They discussed a religion as "animistic," "animatistic," "ancestor worship," "totemic," or as contrasted with "magic," and so on. As the number of more detailed studies of religions increased, two important points were revealed.

First, religions are characterized by an internal complexity; any one system of beliefs and rituals contains elements of several "types"—totemic, magical, animistic, etc. Accordingly, we find that generalizing about a religion by "typing" it is misleading, too simplistic, and obscures the richness and complexity that characterizes it. Methodologically, putting things in boxes and labeling them serves to introduce very low-level order to material that would otherwise be too chaotic and unmanageable. But at the same time this taxonomic approach could obscure the vital issues involved in an empirical problem. Frequently it does not lead beyond the superficial organization of data; it has no explanatory nor predictive value whatsoever.

Second, studies on religious systems have revealed their external variability. As more studies were made in more and different parts of the world, we found that there was tremendous variation in the way beliefs and rituals are expressed. It was felt then that perhaps it is futile to try to look for a common denominator. Emphasis shifted from seeking universals to comparative studies that were culture-specific. Along with this shift in emphasis was a strong trend toward cultural relativism (making judgements about a culture in terms of its own set of standards). The outcome was detailed studies on specific systems, which replaced the global schemes that fit specific "types" into either a linear (evolutionary) scheme or into boxes.

FUNCTIONS OF RELIGION

Malinowski and others asked not what religion *is* but what religions *do* in human life and in social systems. Diverse studies by many anthropologists interested in religion and social organization indicated that religion has various functions.

However, I find it misleading to discuss the function or functions of religion without providing a cautionary note. We have to be aware that any claim that religion has such and such a function presupposes a number of assumptions that usually remain uncontested. For example, as we saw in chapter 2, I discussed Tylor's view that religion has explanatory functions. If we take a closer look at this claim we find that it presupposes that the natives' activities and behavior (and beliefs) are dictated by decisions taken within a purely rational framework. It also assumes that the natives are mystified by certain phenomena that seem unexplainable and that they formulate theories (the theory of the soul) in order to explain such mysterious phenomena. Clearly these are assumptions, and hence do not represent an objectively verified set of facts.

So whenever we talk about the function of religion we are really setting up a hypothesis. This hypothesis must be understood and evaluated within the broader theoretical framework that the anthropologist making the claim takes: "rationalistic," "psychological," "mentalistic," etc. We must consider the set of assumptions that underlies such frameworks.

Nevertheless, in this section I will not explicitly point out the sets of assumptions that underlie the various claimed functions of religion. The discussion is intended, rather, as a synthesis of the basic functions of religion claimed by various anthropologists in different studies. Frequently the premises are more or less obvious.

Religion Explains

First, religion has explanatory functions. We saw how in cases 4, 5, and 7, concepts and beliefs answer the question *why* for a people, whether Zapotec, Nubian, or Trobriand. Spiro says that it can be shown that humans everywhere have a desire to know, to understand, to find meaning. Belief systems provide the members of society with meaning and explanation for otherwise meaningless and inexplicable phenomena.[1] For example, the Azande have a satisfying explanation of why an unfortunate and unusual event took place.

Case 8: Azande Witchcraft.

"It is an inevitable conclusion from Azande descriptions of witchcraft that it is not an objective reality. . . . Witches, as Azande conceive them, cannot exist. The concept of witchcraft nevertheless provides them with a natural philosophy by which the relations between men and unfortunate events are explained and with a ready and stereotyped means of reacting to such events. Witchcraft beliefs also embrace a system of values which regulate human conduct.

Witchcraft is ubiquitous. It plays its part in every activity of Azande life: in agricultural, fishing, and hunting pursuits; in domestic life of homesteads as well as in communal life of district and court; it is an important theme of mental life in which it forms the background of a vast panorama of oracles and magic; its influence is plainly stamped on law and morals, etiquette and religion; it is prominent in technology and language; there is no niche or corner of Azande culture into which it does not twist itself. If blight seizes the groundnut crop it is witchcraft; if the bush is daily scoured for game it is witchcraft; if women laboriously bail water out of a pool and are rewarded by but a few small fish it is witchcraft; if termites do not rise when their swarming is due and a cold useless night is spent in waiting for their flight it is witchcraft; if a wife is sulky and unresponsive to her husband it is witchcraft. . . ."[2]

Religion Validates

Aside from making the world look and feel more sensible to a people, religion has

1. Melford E. Spiro, "Religion: Problems of Definition and Explanation," in *Anthropological Approaches to the Study of Religion* (Association of Social Anthropologists Monographs, no. 3), ed. Michael Banton (London: Tavistock Publications, 1965), p. 110.

2. E. E. Evans-Pritchard, "Witchcraft Explains Unfortunate Events," in *Reader in Comparative Religion*, ed. W. A. Lessa and E. Z. Vogt (New York: Harper & Row, 1965), pp. 440-441.

validating functions. Malinowski has shown how myth functions to legitimize the social order of the Trobriand Islanders.

Case 9: Trobriand Origin Myth.

Members of a Trobriand subclan know, mark, and recount the history of the "hole" from which their ancestress (matrilineal descent) and her brother emerged from the underworld. In that underworld, in the days before life on the earth, men lived as they do now. The ancestral brother and sister brought up with them the sacred objects and knowledge, the skills and crafts, and the magic that distinguish this group from others.

It is brother and sister who emerge because they represent the two essential elements of the subclan; a husband does not emerge because he is, in terms of the subclan, an irrelevant outsider. The ancestral pair live in separate houses because the relationship of brother to sister is marked by sharp taboos.[3] Thus we can see how this Trobriand origin myth validates, justifies and reinforces Trobriand social relations.

Other than providing such direct reinforcement of the social order, Geertz tells us that sacred symbols can function to synthesize a people's ethos—the tone, character, and quality of their life, its moral and aesthetic style and mood, their view of the world, and their ideas of order. Sacred symbols support with powerful sanctions the basic social institutions, values, and goals of a society.[4] A good example is the American flag discussed earlier in case 6.

Case 10: The American Flag, A Sacred Symbol.

There are many strict rules concerning the handling and display of the flag designed to prevent its touching the ground, being stained by other dirt, or being displayed in a "perverted" manner (i.e., upside down or with a nonsymbolic function, as a window or wall drapery—this is the reason for the existence of bunting). It is displayed primarily at five types of occasions: the Fourth of July, election day, Memorial Day, ceremonies of swearing allegiance, and Veterans' Day.

All of these ceremonies emphasize two aspects of citizenship in America: the obligation to sacrifice oneself for the good of American society, and the right of Americans to certain services and goods in exchange for such sacrifices.

Carrying a flag in any protest demonstration *validates* one's action by including it under the rights of citizens. Flying a flag validates a homeowner's ownership of his property, his claim to an entire house for one family, and his eating steak one night each week (or whenever!). Doing these things are part of his right to the pursuit of "happiness" which is guaranteed to all citizens; he has chosen to emphasize his citizenship by displaying the flag. At the same time, however, displaying the flag emphasized the individual's *obligations* to American society. He must pay taxes and even, in times of war, be prepared to sacrifice his life.

Religion Is Psychologically Reinforcing

Humans are constantly confronted with disasters: some are natural such as earthquakes, floods, droughts; some are manmade such as napalm attacks, starvation, etc. There are also the more common everyday tragedies of car accidents, sudden heart attacks, fires, cancer, etc. We are always trying to cope with suffering and problems of good and evil. A people's set of beliefs, whether "scientific," "superhuman," or "sacred," serves in making us feel good while coping.

Kluckhohn was emphasizing this very aspect of religion when he told us that its

3. Bronislaw Malinowski, *Magic, Science, and Religion and Other Essays* (Garden City, New York: Anchor Books, 1954), pp. 111-116.

4. Clifford Geertz, "Religion as a Cultural System," in *Anthropological Approaches to the Study of Religion*, p. 3.

basic function is to provide people with a sense of security in a world that is unpredictable and harsh.[5] In normal, everyday life the sense of security derives from belonging to a group and sharing its beliefs, attitudes, values, and sacred symbols.

In that sense my neighbors in Redondo Beach who in case 2 rejected my child (hence rejected me) were expressing concern that we did not all share the beliefs and attitudes that are the foundation for their sense of security. They felt threatened by a woman in the neighborhood who did not fit their view of "woman": home, children, pregnant. My way of life makes them feel that theirs is *a* way of life instead of *the* way of life. (Perhaps that is also why many American people, including Congress, rejected the National Science Foundation-funded behavioral science course, "Man: A Course of Study," developed as part of its long-standing curriculum improvement program for schools. The course is strongly characterized by a theme of cultural relativism; that is, each culture is seen as uniquely individual because of relevant function and meaning within its setting, neither better nor worse than any other way of doing things. This course clearly tells everybody that "there are other ways of life." It was harshly criticized on the grounds that it exposes students to institutions such as cannibalism, adultery, bestiality, female infanticide, incest, wife-swapping, killing old people, [some of which are not unlike similar middle-class institutionalized behavior in civilized America]. The problem was not so much in the exposure that it provided, but that such institutions are not condemned and presented as a "bad way of life.")

Anthropology is full of cases where the sense of security of certain peoples is shaken to its roots in the face of a perceived threat to their social order. This is particularly dramatized when peoples are invaded by colonialism, exploitation, inequality, etc. They come to realize that theirs was not and is no longer *the* way of life. For example, the Cargo Cults of New Guinea are the people's way of rejecting their "old ways" while the Ghost Dance of American Indians was intended to glorify the "old ways."

There are many other examples in anthropology of peoples in times of stress resorting to religious movements. It is interesting to note that following the frustrating 1967 war between Egypt and Israel, the Egyptian people, the majority of whom are Moslem, witnessed the "return" of the Virgin Mary as she appeared in daylight in Cairo, which in my opinion is not unlike Americans witnessing Unidentified Flying Objects (UFOs) in time of crises. More directly in the religious vein, however, the war in Vietnam has been accompanied by various religious movements in America, "Jesus freaks" being the most popular.

Religion Integrates

Durkheim and Radcliffe-Brown viewed religion and ritual as reinforcing collective sentiment and social integration. Rituals and beliefs are often elaborated around focal points of individual and group experience such as birth, puberty, marriage, death, succession to leadership, warfare, harvest, etc. Some of these are irregular as with death; others are cyclical, as with Christmas, and involve systematic preparation. This latter type is best exemplified in a Saint's Day. I attended the Saint's Day celebrated as *Fiesta de Guadalupe* in the Zapotec community and the Saint's Day celebrated as *Mulid-el-Hassan-wel-Hussein* in Dahmit, Nubia. Both are community rituals involving collective preparation and partic-

5. Clyde Kluckhohn, "Myths and Rituals: A General Theory," *Harvard Theological Review* 35 (1942): 45-79.

ipation. They do in fact bring together members of the whole community. Members, who are otherwise absent for long periods, travel long distances to be with their community on that day. Clearly we find that these rituals serve as integrative devices and provide the solidarity that both Ibn Khaldun and Durkheim told us about.

But a system of beliefs and rituals not only integrates in a social sense, it functions to weave together, as Keesing put it, many segments of the customs and beliefs of a people into an overall conceptual design.[6] That is, religion can function to integrate in a social sense and also in a conceptual sense.

In a very important essay on religion, Clifford Geertz formulates a definition of religion that integrates its functions in a broad framework. "A religion is a system of symbols which acts to establish powerful, pervasive, and long-lasting moods and motivations in men by formulating conceptions of a general order of existence and clothing these conceptions with such an aura of factuality that the moods and motivations seem uniquely realistic."[7]

As cultural patterns, religions give meaning (i.e., collective conceptual form shared by members of a society) to social and psychological reality. They have an intrinsic double aspect: as models of and models for reality. In that sense, religion bridges the gap between reality and the people's ideal view of what reality should be, so that both the nature of the universe and the emotions and motives of people are confirmed and reinforced.[8]

Ritual Stores Information

Leach observes the repetitiveness in ritual behavior. Ritual seems to say the same thing over and over, repeat the same message in many ways and through different channels. He claims that ritual, both verbal and nonverbal, contains information directly related to the social life of a people. It efficiently stores and transmits this information by means of economical sets of symbols. In other words, ritual is one way in which members of a culture encode and communicate relevant cultural information through generations.[9]

Myth and Ritual and Natives' Knowledge

When I analyzed the myths and rituals of the Zapotec I found that they tell us something about what the natives *know*, mostly in an unconscious way, that determines what they say and do. I will demonstrate my framework of analysis in chapter 5. But here I would like to give an example of how ritual constantly activates the implicit ordering of the natives' universe by defining fundamental native concepts. The concept exemplified below is "house."

Case 11: Zapotec House.

The analysis of Zapotec ritual gradually uncovers basic native concepts, as exemplified in the concept of *casa* (house) which reveal a signification on a level deeper than the consciously made statements or activities.

For example, the term *casa* as used by the Zapotec has two different usages on the level of empirical reality. *Casa* may be used to refer to a room built of adobe brick or cement as opposed to other rooms that are made out of bamboo. On the other hand, it is also used to refer to the whole house, including all its rooms, its

6. Roger M. Keesing and Felix M. Keesing, *New Perspectives in Cultural Anthropology* (New York: Holt, Rinehart, and Winston, 1971), p. 303.

7. Clifford Geertz, "Religion as a Cultural System," in *Anthropological Approaches to the Study of Religion*, p. 4.

8. Ibid., pp. 1-46.

9. Edmund R. Leach, "Ritualization in Man in Relation to Conceptual and Social Development," in *Reader in Comparative Religion*, pp. 333-337.

kitchen, its courtyard (*solar*), surrounded by some kind of a fence or a wall.

On the conceptual level, *casa* is defined not by the physical boundary surrounding its courtyard but by the categories of people within it. On this level, *casa* is related to *campo* (field) as a set characterized by binary oppositions and mediation. This will be explained in detail in chapter five. The different significations of house are represented in the diagram below.

For example, in the "dance of the turkey," in the wedding ritual, two men with two live turkeys and two women with two baskets containing ingredients for *mole* (a typical Oaxacan dish of chili and chocolate) are sent in a musical procession by the groom's parents to the houses of the bride's fictive relatives. Around the turkeys' necks hang cigarette packages. All along the road the musical band plays the tune of the "dance of the turkey," and at every intersection each man holds the wings of his turkey and dances with it. Each woman dances holding the basket on her head. This goes on until the procession arrives first at the house of the bride's baptismal godmother. One of the two men delivers his turkey, and one of the two women delivers her basket of *mole* ingredients. Then the baptismal godmother joins the procession, while the second turkey is danced with all the way until the house of the bride's parents. There the second turkey and basket of *mole* ingredients are delivered to the bride's parents, to be delivered eventually by them to the confirmation godmother of the bride. This ends the "dance of the turkey."

Common sense and observation along with native statements clearly attest to the fact that this dance is very exhausting for the people involved, and more so for the two turkeys, since the houses are usually dispersed far away from each other in the village. Moreover, native statements point to the fact that even if the houses do happen to be closer, the procession will still go around the village (that is, by the longer route) before they head to the houses in the sequence indicated earlier. This is particularly curious since it is known from the natives' experience that often the turkeys are delivered dead from exhaustion from the dance.

The question is why do the people go through all of that in order to deliver a raw meal (live turkeys and *mole* ingredients)?

FIGURE 3.1
SIGNIFICATIONS OF HOUSE

Level	House	Signification
1. Empirical	(a) *Casa* (b) *Casa*	Room of Adobe Brick, or Cement House Surrounded by Physical Boundary
2. Conceptual	*Casa*	Concept Opposed to *campo*, Defined and Redefined by Ritual

Indeed there are alternative ways whereby this meal could be delivered.

There is always the alternative way common in most of their ritual where the meal is offered by the *caseros* (people of house) in the house where the ritual takes place. Particularly if, as Lévi-Strauss states, the function of ritual is to "bring about a union . . . an organic relation between two initially separate groups," that is certainly a strange way of doing it.[10] And moreover, it does not necessarily bring about any union.

By taking the *caseros* (in the form of their messengers) all the way to the house of the bride's baptismal godmother and then the house of the bride's parents, ritual is defining (and redefining) the concept *casa* in terms of the categories of people it creates (and recreates) within it. By dancing all over the village from the groom's house to the houses of the bride's fictives, and the house of the bride's parents, ritual extends *casa* beyond its physical boundary to its conceptual boundary.

In other words, these people "know" that house is defined conceptually by drawing a line around the people (categories of relatives) who should be in it. They take their turkey(s) and dance their way to these relatives, drawing that conceptual line. This "knowledge" is at a deeper level of abstraction. They are not conscious of it, and ordinary people from the community will not verbalize this to you. If you ask them why they do that, they will justify such seemingly bizarre behavior by saying the obvious: "we have to deliver the turkey." And if you ask them why do they have to deliver the turkey they will say: "this is a custom; we always deliver a turkey this way in weddings."

For Further Reading

Bateson, Gregory. *Naven.* 2nd ed. Stanford, California: Stanford University Press, 1958. An attempt to discover how a culture systematically organizes the emotions of its members. This involves finding an underlying pattern in the *Naven* ceremonies of the Iatmul of New Guinea and then looking for it in other aspects of their life. An effort to describe the "total culture" in general terms.

Colson, Elizabeth. "Ancestral Spirits and Social Structure among the Tonga." *International Archives of Ethnography* XLVII, Part 1, 1954, pp. 21-68. A demonstration that Tonga beliefs about ancestral spirits reflect various features of their social system and kinship organization; belief and ritual reproduce social realities in the religious sphere.

Evans-Pritchard, E. E. *Witchcraft, Oracles and Magic Among the Azande.* Oxford: Clarendon Press, 1937. A careful description of Azande beliefs and practices in this area which emphasizes ethnographic detail and strives to convince us that witchcraft is the logical product of healthy adult minds, rather than being irrational, paranoid, etc. Yet he does not go beyond merely stating that it is logical; he does not prove it to us by discovering the logical system underlying it, but only shows us the psychological and social functions of the belief in witchcraft. A classic in ethnography, and good reading.

Geertz, Clifford. "Notes on a Balinese Cockfight." *Daedalus,* Winter, 1972, pp. 1-38. A detailed analysis of cockfights as symbols of man's relation to nature, to his emotions, and to his fellow men in Bali. A pleasure to read.

Horton, Robin. "The Kalabari World View: An Outline and Interpretation." *Africa* XXXII, no. 3, 1962, pp. 197-220. An analysis of a Nigerian people's religion in terms of levels, each having a distinct mode of causation that involves spirits of particular types. The highest level, that of a feminine Great Creator, dominates all the others. This system is explained by viewing it as an explanatory

10. Claude Lévi-Strauss, *The Savage Mind* (Chicago: University of Chicago Press, 1966), p. 32.

model comparable to that developed by modern science. A stimulating article, and brief.

Bibliography

Evans-Pritchard, E. E. 1965. "Witchcraft Explains Unfortunate Events." in *Reader in Comparative Religion.* Edited by W. A. Lessa and E. Z. Vogt. New York: Harper & Row, pp. 440-44.

Geertz, Clifford. 1965. "Religion as a Cultural System." In *Anthropological Approaches to the Study of Religion* (Association of Social Anthropologists Monographs no. 3). Edited by Michael Banton. London: Tavistock Publications, pp. 1-46.

Keesing, R. M. and Keesing, F. M. 1971. *New Perspectives in Cultural Anthropology.* New York: Holt, Rinehart, and Winston.

Kluckhohn, Clyde. 1942. "Myths and Rituals: A General Theory." *Harvard Theological Review* 35:45-79.

Leach, Edmund R. "Ritualization in Man in Relation to Conceptual and Social Development." In *Reader in Comparative Religion,* pp. 333-37.

Lévi-Strauss, Claude. 1966. *The Savage Mind.* Chicago: University of Chicago Press.

Malinowski, Bronislaw. 1954. *Magic, Science, and Religion and Other Essays.* Garden City, New York: Anchor Books.

Spiro, Melford E. "Religion: Problems of Definition and Explanation." In *Anthropological Approaches to the Study of Religion,* pp. 85-126.

4 Myth and Ritual

Myth and ritual are the two most significant areas in anthropological studies of religion. The complex and intriguing myths from all over the world regarding the origin and nature of humans, the relationship between man and woman, the origin of culture, and the relationship between humans and their universe have long fascinated anthropologists. They were also equally intrigued by the highly formalized activities, known as rituals, and the rich and varied symbolism associated with them.

Nineteenth-century scholars tended to study myth as separate from rituals. Myths were seen as symbolic descriptions of natural phenomena, closely associated with human questions of how, why, life, death, nature, and so on. One prominent school tried to find an astral basis for all mythic tales. Others, among whom Andrew Lang was prominent, saw in myth a kind of primitive scientific theory. And to early psychoanalysts myths were group fantasies or societal wish fulfillments analogous to dreaming or daydreaming by individuals.

But whether seen as natives' attempts to explain phenomena or, in psychoanalytic terms, as collective dreaming, the interest was in myth as a universal phenomenon and in terms of panhuman symbolic meanings. Associated with that view was an assumption that there is a primacy of myth.

Which Came First, The Myth or the Ritual?

The hypothesis implied in 19th-century studies on myth was that myth came first and that ritual is an enactment of myth. The relationship between myth and ritual was seen in terms of primacy of one over the other. Which one came first? Which one serves as the basis for the other? Hocart questions this whole line of investigation by asking, "If there are myths that give rise to ritual, where do these myths come from?"

The myth theory predominated until 1903, when Jane Harrison saw a clay seal in Greece which showed the Minotaur as actual king of Crete in a bull mask. This observation led her to publish *Prolegomena to the Study of Greek Religion,* which argued that ritual has priority over myth. She reasserted this view more clearly in a later work (1912). Myth arises out of rite, not the reverse; it is the spoken correlative of the acted rite.

Since then the converse of the 19th-century hypothesis that ritual is enactment of myth became established. As study of cross-cultural distribution of myths increased, the ritual hypothesis became more widely accepted. In the words of Boas, "The uniformity of many such rituals over large areas and the diversity of mythological explanations show clearly that the ritual itself is the stimulus for the origin of the myth. . . Ritual existed, and the tale originated . . . to account for it."[1] This ritual theory was supported by many, among whom S. H. Hooke and Lord Raglan were most prominent.

The general thesis of the ritual school is characterized by two main features: (1) myth is the spoken part of ritual; (2) there is no myth without ritual nor ritual without myth.

To recapitulate: two schools emerged out of the interest in the interrelationship between myth and ritual. One says that myth is the ideological projection of ritual and that the purpose of the myth is to provide a foundation for the rite. The other reverses the relationship and regards ritual as a kind of dramatized illustration of the myth.

Who Cares?

However, detailed collection of myths and data on rituals revealed that even though in general we do find rich ritualism and rich mythology together, we also find cases where there is no correspondence between the two. For example, the Toda are reported to have extensive ceremonialism without an equally extensive mythological counterpart. The early Romans seemed to get along very well without mythology. The poverty of the ritual which accompanies the extremely complex mythology of the Mohave is well known. The Bushmen likewise had many myths and very little ritual. The Central Eskimo, where every detail of the Sedna myth has its ritual analogue in rites, are among many examples.

Anthropologists lost interest in the origin issue and functionalists like Kluckhohn found the asserted relationship of primacy between the myth and ritual as too simplistic and inadequate. There is no necessary primacy of myth over ritual, or vice versa. In some cases, myths were composed to justify rituals, but as we have seen in chapter 3, there is a general tendency for the two to be intricately interrelated and to have important functional connections with the social and psychological life of a particular people.

In other words, the attitude was, Who cares? Universalism gave way to particularism. Emphasis shifted to functional studies of myth and ritual in particular societies. The relationship between myth and ritual remained assumed and undiscussed until recently when a fresh outlook by Claude Lévi-Strauss on myth and ritual came to dominate the intellectual climate.

Lévi-Strauss revived interest in the nature of the interrelationship between the two domains in his article "Structure and Dialectics." He says that regardless of whether the myth or the ritual is the original, earlier studies assumed that "they replicate each other; myth exists on the conceptual level and ritual on the level of action." But he goes on to ask if myth and ritual replicate each other, why do they do it so imperfectly? Why doesn't every ritual act out a myth and vice versa? According to Lévi-Strauss:

> "One assumes an orderly correspondence between the two—in other words, a homology. Curiously enough, this homology is demonstrable in only a small number of cases. It remains to be seen why all myths do not correspond to rites and vice versa, and most important, why there should be such a curious replication in the first place. I intend to show by means of a concrete example that this homology does not always exist; or, more specifically, that when we do find such a homology, it might very well constitute a particular illustration of a more generalized relationship between myth and ritual and between the

1. Franz Boas, *The Mind of Primitive Man*, 2nd ed. (New York: Macmillan Co., 1938), p. 617.

rites themselves. Such a generalized relationship would imply a one-to-one correspondence between the elements of rites which seem to differ, or between the elements of any one rite and any one myth. Such a correspondence could not, however, be considered a homology."

We will see, however, that Lévi-Strauss does not look for a correspondence between myth and ritual in a *single society,* nor is he talking about myth and ritual as idealizations defined by anthropologists for the purposes of cross-cultural comparison. Rather, he looks at myth and ritual within a particular cultural area, which includes societies known to be historically and culturally related. He begins his demonstration by choosing a Pawnee myth, which he labels the "myth of the pregnant boy," and comparing it to rituals from the Blackfoot, Mandan, and Hidatsa, all neighbors of the Pawnee.

"An ignorant young boy becomes aware that he possesses magical powers that enable him to cure the sick. Jealous of the boy's increasing reputation, an old medicine man of established position visits him on several different occasions, accompanied by his wife. Enraged because he obtains no secret in exchange for his own teachings, the medicine man offers the boy a pipe filled with magical herbs. Thus bewitched, the boy discovers that he is pregnant. Full of shame, he leaves his village and seeks death among wild animals. The animals, moved to pity by his misfortune, decide to cure him. They extract the fetus from his body. They teach him their magical powers, by means of which the boy, on returning to his home, kills the evil medicine man and becomes himself a famous and respected healer."

This summary of what is really a very long story is enough to provide illustrations of the following contrasts or oppositions:

"(1) *initiated shaman versus noninitiated shaman,* that is, the opposition between acquired power and innate power; (2) *child* versus *old man,* since the myth insists on the youth of one protagonist and the old age of the other; (3) *confusion of sexes* versus *differentiation of sexes;* all of Pawnee metaphysical thought is actually based on the idea that at the time of creation of the world antagonistic elements were intermingled and that the first work of the gods consisted in sorting them out. The young child is asexual or, more accurately, the male and female principles coexist in him. Conversely, in the old man the distinction is irrevocable—an idea clearly expressed in the myth by the fact that his wife is always with him—in contrast with the boy, who is alone but who harbors in himself both masculinity and femininity (he becomes pregnant); (4) *fertility of the child* (despite his virginity) versus *sterility of the old man* (notwithstanding his constantly mentioned marriage)."

These same oppositions can be found in other Pawnee myths which are variants of the "pregnant boy" theme. The myths are not alike *in detail;* for instance, in one variant the boy becomes "pregnant" with a magically expanding ball of clay. Yet the opposition "confusion of sexes/differentiation of sexes" still stands, as symbolized by a pregnant boy and a married couple who are distinct in sex. Comparing different versions helps separate trivial material from the significant oppositions common to them all. Once he has done this for Pawnee myths, Lévi-Strauss is ready to look for corresponding oppositions in Pawnee ritual.

But he finds none. Among the Pawnee, shamanistic societies are not divided into age-grades, and initiation as a shaman does not involve a ritual of passage from a junior age-grade to a senior one. Hence the opposition youth/age is not present, nor is the idea of confusion of the sexes in the body of a youth. Among the Pawnee the student is initiated as a shaman by his teacher; but in their myth the boy, who is already a shaman by virtue of his *innate* power, is *refused* initiation by an older man who did *not* teach him. Here ritual is the *reverse* of myth. If *all* of the myth were reversed by ritual in this way we could say that myth and ritual were related through inversion, but as we have seen the initiation ritual simply lacks some of the (supposedly corresponding) myth's most important oppositions and so we must look at other ritual activities to see if we can find these missing elements.

This is what Lévi-Strauss does when he examines the ritual of shaman initiation among other Plains Indian peoples.

"Among these tribes, societies are based on age-grades. The transition from one to another is achieved by purchase, and the relationship between seller and buyer is conceived as a relationship between "father" and "son." Finally, the candidate always appears in the company of his wife, and the central motif of the transaction is the handing over of the "son's" wife to the "father," who carries out with her an act of real or symbolic coitus, which is, however, always represented as a fertility act."

Bear in mind, here, that it is the "*son*" who is ritually being fertilized, or initiated, even though this takes place through the "son's" wife. Hence the "son's" wife acts as both a woman and a "son" of the shaman "father" in this ritual situation. It is *she* who combines aspects of both sexes in her person in this case, not a "pregnant boy." Once this is recognized it is clear that all the other oppositions present in the Pawnee myth are to be found in the Mandan ritual.

FIGURE 4.1

INVERTED SYMMETRY OF MYTH AND RITUAL

	Pawnee Myth	Plains Indian Ritual
Initiated/Noninitiated	Old Man/Boy	Boy/Old Man
Young/Old	Boy/Man and Woman	"Son" and His Wife/"Father"
Confusion of Sexes/ Differentiation of Sexes	Male, Female Boy/ Husband and Wife	Woman Who is "Son" *and* Sex Partner to "Father"/Initiate Who is Husband to a Wife
Fertility/Sterility	Boy/Old Man	Old Man/Boy

Furthermore, we can see that for three out of four oppositions, the roles of the actors are *reversed.* (In the case of confusion of sexes/differentiation of sexes, the ambiguous role is given to another of the three principal actors.) Lévi-Strauss comments:

"We could further pursue these comparisons, which would all lead to the same conclusion, namely, that the Pawnee myth reveals a ritual system which is the reverse, not of that prevailing among the Pawnee, but of a system which they do not employ and which exists among related tribes whose ritual organization is exactly the opposite of that of the Pawnee."

He goes on to compare these two to another Plains Indian ritual, the *hako,* which is done to formalize the alliance of two groups. An actor of ambiguous sex, as well as all of the oppositions already named, can also be found here. In the end, Lévi-Strauss concludes that the Pawnee myth and the two Plains Indian rituals are all alike because they establish the oppositions man/woman, father/son and then *equate* the two. We can see that in both the myth and the ritual a "father" treats his "son" like a man treats a woman. This equation may be a reflection of the kinship terminology of these peoples. A Mandan man calls his wife's brothers by a term which also means "father"; they call him "son." Thus their terminology equates marriage (man/woman) with descent (father/son).[2]

Now, how does all this relate to our question? Why doesn't every ritual correspond to a myth? Lévi-Strauss seems to be saying that this lack of correspondence for a particular society is a matter of historical accident. Each single society, when borrowing myths and rites or maintaining them from one generation to the next, does not necessarily choose them as "matched sets" from the body of myths and rites in its cultural environment. Also, when they borrow a myth or rite they can invert or permutate its elements to their taste, as long as the key oppositions and the statement important for the larger culture area are still expressed. This implies that, for a given cultural area, myth and ritual *do* correspond to each other, because at this stage they will be products of the same underlying sets of oppositions which generate both myth and ritual structures, *not* because myth and ritual necessarily "come in twos." The relation between a myth and a ritual is, in Lévi-Strauss's view, essentially the same as the relation between two myths or two rituals from the same cultural environment. *Both* myth and ritual become meaningful when we set up the logical oppositions important to a culture and then relate these oppositions to each other. Both myth and ritual "work" according to the same principles.

But we are getting ahead of ourselves. Lévi-Strauss has spent very little time relating myth to ritual; most of his work deals only with myth. Before we can discuss this, it is best to see how other anthropologists have treated myth.

MYTH

William Bascom observes that all human groups known to us have some form of oral tradition but that not all forms are myths. He, and others, distinguish several types of oral tradition, the most important of which are myths and legends.

The Taxonomic Approach

The major characteristic that distinguishes myths from other types is their importance in the religious system. In addition, myths are considered to be truthful

2. Claude Lévi-Strauss, "Structure and Dialectics," in *Structural Anthropology* (New York: Basic Books, 1963), pp. 232-241.

accounts of past happenings. They are accepted on faith, sacred in character, and often associated with the ritual (religious) system of the society.[3]

The above traits were criticized on the basis that they are difficult to detect. That is, for us to find out whether a form of oral tradition is myth or not, we have to investigate and dig into past history. Moreover, there is the difficulty of identifying "sacredness" in a tale to label it myth.

Other characteristics were suggested to help distinguish myth from legend. The main characters in myth are usually not human in the ordinary sense. They are animals, superhumans, or culture heroes with magical powers, mostly characters which combine contradictory features and thus appear ambiguous or anomalous. They are usually neither strictly human nor strictly animal, not strictly male nor strictly female. Moreover, myths are invariably removed from the present world either in time or in space. They are either placed in the distant past or in a totally different world, as for example, the sky world, the spirit world, or the world of the dead. Some myths give explanations of how present customs came to be, while others purport to justify the details of existing religious rituals.

Like myths, legends are thought to be true. However, legends differ from myths in that they relate historical events within the present world, and within a shorter time span. The characters are human beings. Legends do not purport to sanctify customs and social rules; they are simply descriptions of past events.

But pigeonholing forms of oral tradition (or anything else) in boxes is not a very productive exercise in anthropology. Many saw the futility of this taxonomic approach and the similar attempt of "defining" specific kinds of narratives as myths. Most felt that myth should be used as a convenient label for the whole range of narrative styles and forms of oral tradition. Myth is simply a "sacred" tale. Let me give you a favorite Zapotec myth from my work in Oaxaca as an example.

Case 12: The Matlazigua Myth.

"It's happened to several people; to several people the *matlazigua* appeared, sure, María Sanchez. She looks beautiful and just like your lover, the girl next door. That's how she is. The woman (*matlazigua*), she'll talk to you and then manage to seduce you. Afterwards, when the man arises in the morning, he is (*jodido*) exhausted, and he dies. Well, he dies, then, unless he confides in a friend [so that] he [the friend] can go and get his *machete* [penis] for him. You see he [the friend] has his *misterio*, he has his *misterio*, yes he has his *misterio*. He is aware [of how to go about doing things].

Sometimes he [the victim] will die because of not confiding in someone about what happened.

There is this man Camilo, it happened to him once, up over there in the field, he took his animals and sat down in the shade, and sleep overtook him. Then when he woke up, already he was disarmed [his penis was gone]. Already when he arrived home he had a temperature and he was dying. And as he is my *consuegro*, immediately I learned what had happened, and I went to see. Well, I say to him, 'what happened?'

'Well,' he said, 'this and that and the other, and now what do you think is the problem with me? A very high temperature, and the way it happened, listen. I was watching the animals over there, and I sat under a tree, and in this way sleep overtook me. When I woke up, I was already confused and I felt that I had to drive the animals back home.'

Well, I had come to see Camilo and found that he no longer could perform sexually the way we do. 'Can I touch it,' I asked. 'Why not,

3. William Bascom, "The Forms of Folklore," *Journal of American Folklore* 78 (1965):3-20.

sure,' he answered. Then I touched it, and I said, 'Uh, the *matlazigua* disarmed you for sure Feel it yourself and you'll see.' He got really frightened. 'If you want we can do something about it,' I told him. 'Go ahead,' he said. 'I'm going,' I told him, 'lend me a guitar [in the old days it used to be *viguela*], a bottle of mescal (or *aguardiente*), a pack of cigarettes and a deck of cards. I'm going now and I'll be back.'

Well, I left the house about ten at night and went to where it happened, over there somewhere in the field where the *chingadera* (sex) took place. Fine, fine. When I arrived there it was just the right time to begin working. I sat there, I spread out my blanket, I began to tune my guitar. I began to play it, although I don't know how to play except to make a nice sound and that is all, a few notes. Well, there I was under a tree and before I realized it I was in the palace of the chief of the *matlazigua,* the horned one himself, the devil.

'Come in friend,' I was told. 'What happened that you arrived here?' he asked. 'Well, friend, pardon my arrival, but first let's drink what I have brought,' I told him. I told him this and that and the other thing. There are only seven words that you say, and I said, 'and the penis is here.' I continued, 'It's those cursed girls. My *consuegro* was sleeping.'

Of course I could recognize the *machete.* Over there are many, many *machetes* of specific persons. One can tell the fresh penis from the old penises. The old ones are dried out. Their men have died. But a fresh one is easy to find and point out. So I found the penis, took it and returned to my *consuegro's* house.

There I lifted the blanket and stuck the little pistol [penis] in its place. 'Okay, now,' I told my *consuegro,* 'cover yourself now. Let's go to it . . . joy, mescal, and all that.' Within half an hour Camilo's temperature had returned to normal. 'How do you feel?' I asked him. 'Already I'm better, fine, nothing (bad) is happening,' he said. 'Be very careful', I told him. 'Don't you go and sleep in the fields, because there are bad hours, as much at night as in the daytime; there is evil in the daytime and evil at night. These evil airs, the *matlaziguas,* move about and naturally wherever the opportunity arises they will disarm you [steal your penis].

When such a thing happens I can aid those who need it, to whom it happens. It happened to the *difunto* Jaruso, this black person who lives over there. It happened in the crossroads intersection of El Chamizal. In this case a beautiful woman appeared to him and got his attention. He jumped to the side of the fields and stayed talking and chatting with her, and so on and so forth.

Following that he got a very high fever. As *mayor de vara* he was on his way to the *municipio* when the *matlazigua* appeared. When he went to the *municipio* offices his fever was high, but because he was ashamed (*vergüenza*) to tell what had happened he didn't talk to anyone about his experience. Well, in three days he died. And why? Simply because he didn't tell anyone what had happened. He died from (*vergüenza*) shame."[4]

As a major alternative to the taxonomic approach, a school emerged that strongly advocated the notion that myths should be seen and examined in the context of ethnographic background and in relationship to all the other domains in a cultural system. Those who hold that view feel that myths are contextual and therefore cannot be analyzed as independent entities. This approach strongly rejects earlier attempts of looking at myth for its meaning on its own merits and any notions that myths are intellectual explanatory devices or symbolic descriptions of natural phenomena. Two significant perspectives within that broad approach are Myth As Charter and Myth As Culture-Reflector.

4. This case was provided by a Zapotec informant, Martin Hernandez, and was collected and translated from the Zapotec into Spanish by Abel Hernandez. The English translation is mine.

Myth As Charter

In his classic work, "Myth in Primitive Psychology," Bronislaw Malinowski accomplished two things: he disposed of the notion that myth can be treated as an iso ated phenomenon, while creating a totally new framework for myth analysis. His work drew attention to the significance of oral tradition (generally neglected in earlier works) as an integral part of social life.

On the basis of his long-term and intensive field work in the Trobriand Islands, Malinowski claimed that myth is a "charter for belief"; it serves as sacred legitimizer for a'l that people think, say, or do. To understand myth the observer must understand native social organization. The origin story of a people is in fact the legal charter of their society.

Malinowski strongly reacted against the position that myths are elaborate networks of symbols centered on one or another natural phenomenon. He equally rejected any theories that intellectualize myth. He says that his own fieldwork among the Trobriands shows the people to be extremely pragmatic and responsive to basic survival needs. Myth for the natives is an extremely important social force direct'y relevant to their pragmatic interests. Myth is not symbolic; it is a direct expression of its subject matter.

Myth, Malinowski argues, expresses, enhances, and codifies belief, vouches for the efficacy of ritual, and contains practical rules for man's guidance. As such it is a pragmatic charter of primitive faith and moral wisdom. By looking at myth as intellectual endeavour, theorists make it a rational process of reasoning, ignoring the emotional, entertaining, and functional aspects of myth, but most importantly its deep connection to social values.[5]

If we go back to the *matlazigua* myth in case 12 and look at it from a Malinowskian view, we find that it tells us the following:

(a) The field is dangerous; evil things happen there.

(b) One should not sleep in the field.

(c) One should not fall for illicit sexual temptations.

(d) One should confide in relatives.

(e) One should ask for help when he needs it.

(f) Beautiful women are seductive and related to the Devil.

Thus one approach considers myth as a literal guide to behavior. Other anthropologists look at myth as reflecting cultural content.

Myth As Culture-Reflector

Whereas the Malinowskian position of myth as charter focuses more on the function of myth within a holistic totality, the culture-reflector school pays more attention to the content of the mythical text itself.[6] However, the content in that framework is only meaningful within the context of ethnographic information outside the mythological realm. An extreme position within that framework is that which seeks a literal interpretation of myth as providing a chronicle of actual events. In other words, we look in myth for a reflection of cultural content that might otherwise escape our attention as anthropologists, or as confirmation of the empirical reality that interests the anthropologist. An example from my research in Nubia can clarify how certain ethnographic facts are reflected in mythical beliefs.

Case 13: *There Are More Females in the River.*
In a paper called "Ritual and the River in

5. Bronislaw Malinowski, *Myth in Primitive Psychology* (New York: W. W. Norton & Co., 1926).

6. William A. Lessa and Evon Z. Vogt, eds., *Reader in Comparative Religion,* 3rd ed. (New York: Harper & Row, 1972), pp. 249, 251.

Dahmit," I describe the overwhelming importance of the river Nile in the lives of the Nubian people. Dahmiti life would literally come to a halt without the Nile. It plays a crucial part in Dahmiti economic life, as medium of human transport, as communication means, as channel for commerce, and as the only source of water for drinking, washing, bathing, and so on.

Along with its general importance we find that stress is put upon the place of the river in the Dahmiti religious system. It plays a significant part in the Dahmiti system of rituals and beliefs.

Dahmitis believe that the river is inhabited by anthropomorphous beings called *dogri*. *Dogri* are both male and female. The females are referred to as *Banat Es-Saliheen* (Daughters of the Virtuous or Pious), and when visible appear naked, with long straight hair, vertical eyes and eyebrows, and very long breasts which are thrown crosswise over their shoulders. The males are *Welad Es-Saliheen* (Sons of the Virtuous or Pious). However, a definite picture of them could not be given.

What is important is that *Banat Es-Saliheen* are said to outnumber *Welad Es-Saliheen* because the river "prefers females." A culture-reflector position is appropriate here when we look at the actual ethnographic situation of the Dahmiti.

Because of the increase in river elevation caused by the Aswan Dam, agriculture was becoming scarcer and men from Dahmit began to seek employment in the urban centers of Cairo and Alexandria. Urban migration continued to increase, and the result was that the community of Dahmit, and many others like it in Egyptian Nubia, became predominantly female.

So the "myth" of the *dogri* reflects culture because Dahmit too "prefers women" in the sense that women outnumber the resident men by about 70 percent.[7] The myth reflects the actual demographic situation in Dahmit.

This extreme position, however, is not very common among anthropologists. As William Lessa warns us in his paper "Discoverer-of-the-Sun," we should not assume that myths reflect an exact image of the culture that produces them. Frequently the information they do supply is fragmentary and not at all a true mirror of a culture's totality. They incorporate elements of culture selectively.

Instead, Lessa demonstrates in his analysis of Ulithi mythical text that myth should be considered in light of complementary ethnographic information.[8] In simple words, a less extreme culture-reflector position says the content of myth does tell us something about a people's culture, but not everything. It should be seen as complementary to other ethnographic information.

Both views of "myth as charter" and "myth as culture-reflector" insist that the myths of a people be analyzed in their social context. To treat the myths without looking at their ethnographic background would give us distorted meaning and function.

Not so, says Claude Lévi-Strauss, who opened new frontiers for the analysis of myths as logical models with structure and meaning in their own right, rather than as reflections and projections.

Myth As Logical Model

Looking at myth as a logical model is part of a broader theoretical framework called structuralism, whose leading exponent is French anthropologist Claude Lévi-Strauss. At the risk of oversimplification I will define the basics of this framework in terms of the four fundamental premises

7. Fadwa El Guindi, "Ritual and the River in Dahmit," in *Contemporary Egyptian Nubia*, vol. 2, ed. Robert A. Fernea (New Haven, Conn.: HRAF Press, 1966), pp. 239-256.

8. William A. Lessa, "Discoverer-of-the-Sun," in *Reader in Comparative Religion*, eds. W. A. Lessa and E. Z. Vogt (New York: Harper & Row, 1972), pp. 251-269.

formulated by the founder of structural linguistics, N. Trubetzkoy. They are:

(1) The object of study is unconscious infrastructure rather than conscious phenomena.

(2) The basis of analysis is the relations between terms; terms are not to be treated as independent entities.

(3) The area of investigation is to be conceived of as representing a system.

(4) The goal of the research is to discover general laws.

Decades of worldwide anthropological investigations revealed immense variation in the content of cultural products. That is, the products of culture are enormously varied, and when the anthropologist compares Arab Bedouin, Tuareg, Nubians, and the Zapotec she is first struck and fascinated by the differences. We find that people from different places do all kinds of things in different ways.

But we also discovered that there are limits to diversity. It is the human mind that generates these cultural artifacts. This mind structures reality and imposes form on content. Since all cultures are the product of human brains there must be, beneath the surface, properties that are universal. Lévi-Strauss is interested in these universal properties and sees them as expressions of underlying principles of the mind. To discover these principles and understand them he looks at the structuring of cultural domains created and recreated by these principles. One such domain is myth.

Myth is especially appropriate for structuralists interested in the human mind because it is an area where free, unrestrained, creative human thinking is expressed. There are many imaginable forms of marriage, house styles, residence patterns. But we will not actually find them all in human societies because too many constraints prevent their actualization.

There are limiting factors—ecological, technological, physical, or whatever—that make the realization of an infinite number of human creations impossible.

But humans can *think* all of the conceivable possibilities; and in myth human thought is at its freest. As Lévi-Strauss says: "With myth everything becomes possible." So looking at actual mythical content we get the impression of tremendous variety of trivial incident, associated with a great deal of repetition, which leaves us with a sense of randomness and arbitrariness. Too much is said, and what is said appears without order and seems to follow no logic.

However, examination of many different myths collected in widely different regions shows, as Lévi-Strauss puts it, "astounding similarity." So he asks the question: "If the content of a myth is contingent, how are we going to explain the fact that myths throughout the world are so similar?"[9]

By this question he throws out the notion that myths are meaningful only within their cultural context, and shifts our attention to the inherent logic in myth that accounts for universal similarity.

In so many words, Lévi-Strauss is saying that society is a machine for the exchange of information. This exchange is made possible by the fact that social phenomena such as language, myth, ritual, etc. are structured. As anthropologists we are interested in examining the structuring of these phenomena to uncover the code through which the exchange of information actually takes place. A well-known example of a system based on a binary structure is the Morse code, which utilizes a distinction between short and long dashes. We will see shortly that Lévi-Strauss in a somewhat more complex fashion also bases his ana'yses of culture on a binary op-

9. Claude Lévi-Strauss, "The Structural Study of Myth," in *Structural Anthropology* (New York: Basic Books, 1963), p. 208.

position. The implication that follows from Lévi-Strauss's work is that this binary property is determined by processing requirements within the human brain.

Structural linguistics seems to confirm this binary perspective. In his structural approach, Lévi-Strauss draws on significant findings in linguistics, but particularly that of the Prague School in phonology. Phonology is the system of abstract units that describe the sound system of a language.

Linguistics holds that structures are formed by units (of sound) related to each other on the basis of features in opposition. This was first proposed in the Prague school of linguistics by Trubetzkoy and was developed by Jakobson and Halle, and later by Chomsky and Halle.[10]

Trubetzkoy conceptualized the unit of sound, which he called a phoneme, in terms of sound contrasts seen as a bundle of distinctive features. A contrast in polarity for some feature is called opposition. Roman Jakobson stressed the notion that distinctive features are in strictly *binary opposition* to one another.

To understand this framework better, let us first consider some examples in detail from the English sound system. In English, the sounds represented by the letters *d* and *t* differ on the basis of one feature, that of voicing. Voicing is a physical property created by the vibration of the vocal cords in what is sometimes called the Adam's apple: *d* is voiced; *t* is unvoiced. You can feel the difference if you say the two sounds with your fingers on the front of your throat. Voicing therefore is a distinctive feature which separates *d* from *t*; *d* is + voice, *t* is − voice. Thus *t* and *d* are *in opposition* in regards to the feature of *voice*.

On the other hand, the sounds represented by *d* and *n* also differ on the basis of one feature, but not the same feature of voicing. The feature distinguishing *d* and *n* is nasality: *n* is made by allowing the air to resonate in the nose or nasal cavity. Accordingly, *n* is + nasal, *d* is − nasal. We can represent these differences with the following matrix:

FIGURE 4.2
ENGLISH SOUNDS AND DISTINCTIVE FEATURES

	Voicing	Nasality
d	+	−
t	−	−
n	+	+

Thus we find that the fundamental units of the system of English sounds are made up of polar features. Each unit is distinguished from every other unit by a difference in value in one or more distinctive features. I say "fundamental" units or "fundamental" differences because some differences are more superficial. For example, *t* and *d* also differ from each other in that when *t* is the first sound in an English word it is accompanied by a puff of air called aspiration; *d* has no such aspiration.

You can check this by holding the back of your hand about an inch from your mouth

10. N. S. Trubetzkoy, *Principles of Phonology* (translation of *Grundzüge der Phonologie*, Travaux du Cercle Linguistique de Prague, 7, 1939), trans. Christiane A. M. Baltaxe (Berkeley: University of California Press, 1969); Roman Jakobson and Morris Halle, *Fundamentals of Language* (The Hague: Mouton & Co., 1956); Noam Chomsky and Morris Halle, *The Sound Pattern of English* (New York: Harper & Row, 1968).

while saying "dill" and "till." This aspiration is not present for all instances of *t*. For example, it does not occur when *t* follows *s* as in "still." Moreover, the feature of aspiration is not distinctive in English. The word "till" pronounced without aspiration would still be recognized as "till" in English.

It is important to note that not all languages recognize the same set of fundamental distinctions. For example, while aspiration is a superficial (or phonetic) difference in English, it is a fundamental (or phonemic) distinction in Thai. Pronouncing a Thai word with an aspirated or unaspirated *t* will signal two completely different words with different meanings to a speaker of Thai.

On the other hand, a fundamental English distinction like voicing is not fundamental in many of the world's languages, so that speakers of some languages, as for example Arabic, will take *p* and *b* to be essentially the same sound. Perhaps you have heard Arabs saying "bebber" for "pepper."

Correspondingly, Lévi-Strauss claims that if there is meaning to be found in mythology, it cannot reside in the isolated elements that make up the content of a myth, but in the way these elements are combined, i.e., in the specific way in which these elements relate to the system that is being expressed in the myth.

Myth is made up of constituent units called mythemes. For example, to go back to the Pawnee myth (discussed earlier), we can consider "pregnant boy" a mytheme that is + youth, + confusion of sexes, and − initiated, etc. Mythemes are not isolated relations; they are bundles of such relations. It is only as bundles that these relations can be put to use and combined so as to produce meaning.

Structural analysis requires that we identify and isolate these units. By systematically doing that to all the known variants of a particular myth, it becomes possible to organize them into a set forming a permutation group.

In other words, every myth is a variation on some theme. This theme is expressed by a combination of mythemes; and we can discover mythemes by comparing many similar myths rather than isolating one variant (version) and focusing on it. In that sense, all versions of a myth are seen as "correct" versions.

The examples discussed above illustrate several of the basic premises taken from Trubetzkoy and used by Lévi-Strauss in his analysis of myth. First, the description of a set of phenomena is best treated as being part of a system. Second, terms or units are not independent entities. The basis of their analysis is the relations between units. Third, what is perceived as being important and significant is determined by the frequently unconscious system of the perceiver. Fourth, it is important to discover the general laws that form part of the system.

As an example of this last point let us return to the English aspirated *t*. We find that both *p* and *k*, which can be shown to be in the same class of sounds as *t*, are also subject to the rule of aspiration as it applies to *t*. Thus the aspiration phenomenon in English is a general law or rule that applies across a class of sounds (as described by a specific set of distinctive features) and not unique to the single sound *t*.

Lévi-Strauss demonstrates concretely his method of structural analysis by using the Oedipus myth. It is probably so well-known that it is not necessary to state its text. Lévi-Strauss proceeds to isolate the mythemes in Oedipus. Then he tries out several arrangements of these mythemes until he finds one arrangement that corresponds most to the principles discussed earlier. The chart of Lévi-Strauss's own arrangement is on page 37.

This chart tells us that there are four vertical columns, each of which includes several relations belonging to the same bundle. All the relations belonging to the same column exhibit one common feature which, Lévi-Strauss says, "it is our task to discover." "For instance, all the events grouped in the first column on the left have something to do with blood relations which are overemphasized,

FIGURE 4.3
OEDIPUS MYTH AS SETS OF RELATIONS

Cadmos Seeks His Sister Europa, Ravished by Zeus			
	The Spartoi Kill One Another	Cadmos Kills the Dragon	
	Oedipus Kills His Father, Laios		Labdacos (Laios's Father) = *Lame* (?) Laios (Oedipus's Father) = *Left-Sided* (?)
		Oedipus Kills the Sphinx	
			Oedipus = *Swollen-Foot*(?)
Oedipus Marries His Mother, Jocasta			
	Eteocles Kills His Brother, Polynices		
Antigone Buries Her Brother Polynices, Despite Prohibition			

that is, are more intimate than they should be. Let us say, then, that the first column has as its common feature the *overrating of blood relations*. It is obvious that the second column expresses the same thing, but inverted: *underrating of blood relations*. The third column refers to monsters being slain. As to the fourth, *names, precisely because they are used as such*, are a common feature: *difficulties in walking straight and standing upright*."

Then, Lévi-Strauss considers the two columns on the right. He asks: What is the relationship between them?

"Column three refers to monsters. The dragon is a chthonian being which has to be killed in order that mankind be born from the Earth; the Sphinx is a monster unwilling to permit men to live. The last unit reproduces the first one, which has to do with the *autochthonous origin* of mankind. Since the monsters are overcome by men, we may thus say that the common feature of the third column is *denial of the autochthonous origin of man*.

This immediately helps us to understand the meaning of the fourth column. In mythology it is a universal characteristic of men born from the Earth that at the moment they emerge from the depth they either cannot walk or they walk clumsily. This is the case of the chthonian beings in the mythology of the Pueblo: Muyingwu, who leads the emergence, and the chthonian Shumaikoli are lame ("bleeding-foot," "sore-foot"). The same happens to the Koskimo of the Kwakiutl after they have been swallowed by the chthonian monster, Tsiakish: When they returned to the surface of the earth "they limped forward or tripped sideways." Thus the common feature of the fourth column is the *persistence of the autochthonous origin of man*."

To recapitulate the features that characterize all the columns—

column one: overrating of blood relations;

column two: underrating of blood relations;

column three: denial of the autochthonous origin of man;

column four: persistence of the autochthonous origin of man.

On examining these four features, we detect a logical relationship between them. Column four is to column three as column one is to column two. Thus in equation form:

column 4 : column 3 :: column 1 : column 2.

Lévi-Strauss concludes:

"Turning back to the Oedipus myth, we may now see what it means. The myth has to do with the inability, for a culture which holds the belief that mankind is autochthonous, to find a satisfactory transition between this theory and the knowledge that human beings are actually born from the union of man and woman. Although the problem obviously cannot be solved, the Oedipus myth provides a kind of logical tool which relates the original problem—born from one or born from two?—to the derivative problem: born from different or born from same? By a correlation of this type, the overrating of blood relations is to the underrating of blood relations as the attempt to escape autochthony is to the impossibility to succeed in it. Although experience contradicts theory, social life validates cosmology by its similarity of structure. Hence cosmology is true."[11]

RITUAL

Is there structure in ritual? Yes. This is exactly what I am working on in my analysis of Zapotec ritual. But not everybody is looking for a structure in ritual. Some are more interested in its rich symbolism. Others claim they are looking for a structure but

11. Claude Lévi-Strauss, "The Structural Study of Myth," in *Structural Anthropology* (New York: Basic Books, 1963), pp. 214-217.

continue to look for it in the wrong place. We have learned from Lévi-Strauss and the whole school of structuralism that if we remain on the ground we can only deal with *content;* structure will elude us. First, however, let me explain what I mean by these two terms.

Content refers to individual elements (of myth, of a work of art, of a rite, etc.) as opposed to the relationship *between* such elements, or structure. Structure is *always* abstract, being an order imposed on objects, but content can be concrete *or* abstract.

Picture a line of milk bottles on your doorstep. The milk bottles (content) can be touched (are *concrete*) but the *line* in which they are standing cannot. The numbers 1, 2, 3, 4, 5, . . . 12 are *abstractions* but also can be arranged to form the same structure as milk bottles can form: a line. Similarly, milk bottles can be arranged in a circle, and numbers can be pictured as arranged to make a clock face. When an airline pilot is told that the airport lies ten miles ahead, he knows that he must continue in a *straight line,* passing 3 miles, 5 miles, etc. until he reaches 10. But if he is told that the landing is at ten o'clock (a west-northwesterly direction, for example), he knows he must turn the plane until it faces that direction. We can see that the number ten means nothing if it is not related to other such numbers by a structure; on the other hand, no structure can exist without elements, and if those elements are not identified, the structure (in this case a line or a circle) tells us nothing specific. You cannot interpret structure without studying its content (whether concrete or abstract).[12] From this example we can see that those critics of Lévi-Strauss who find fault with him for "studying *only* structure" have failed to grasp the relationship between content and structure in his analysis.

In the case of ritual, we find that structure is the underlying system that relates rites and symbols to one another. This system is *unconscious,* that is, it cannot be fully verbalized by native informants even while they are acting in conformity to its rules. Because of this we must look for it at a very abstract level. And it is at this level rather than that of superficial content that the significant message is conveyed.

What is Ritual?

Like myth and other cultural domains ritual had its share of being defined and classified. Gluckman suggested that ritual must be distinguished from ceremony. Ceremony is an organization of human activity that involves the playing out of social relations which cannot be expressed informally. Ritual involves the change of a person's status while relating that person to the supernatural.[13]

Turner supports this distinction but defines ritual and ceremony somewhat differently and more clearly than Gluckman. He sees both of them as forms of religious behavior; ritual is associated with social transition, thus "transformative," while ceremony is associated with social status, thus "confirmatory."[14] However, this distinction did not hold up consistently and is ignored in most analyses. In addition, we find ritual also being classified as religious and magical, calendrical and critical, sacred and secular, private and public, sacrificial, totemic, political, economic, and so on. I will single out and elaborate on one type or class of rit-

12. I thank W. C. Young for providing this example.

13. Max Gluckman, *Politics, Law and Ritual in Tribal Society* (Chicago: Aldine Publishing Co., 1965), p. 251.

14. Victor Turner, "Betwixt and Between: the Liminal Period in *Rites de Passage,*" in *Reader in Comparative Religion,* eds. W. A. Lessa and E. Z. Vogt (New York: Harper & Row, 1972), pp. 338-339.

ual because it represents a significant step beyond mere pigeonholing. This type is "rites of passage."

"Rites de Passage"

Arnold van Gennep is the scholar who analytically isolated a set of ritual called rites of passage because of its distinctive internal organization.[15] He defined *"rites de passage"* as "rites which accompany every change of place, state, social position, and age." His contribution lies in his discovery of a recurring pattern found in rites of passage all over the world. Persons passing from one status to another, as for example from civilian status to military status when one joins the U. S. army or from single status to married status in tribal society, have to go through three successive phases: separation; margin (or limen); and incorporation or aggregation.

The first phase of separation is symbolically represented by behavior or activity that indicates detachment of the particular individual or group from a previous structural position. The second phase is a marginal period. The ritual subject is neither in the previous state nor in the new one; it is an in-between stage of liminality.

Victor W. Turner, who uses van Gennep's framework in organizing his own data on the Ndembu in Zambia, feels that this liminal period needs to be more closely examined because it is "rich in symbolism and culturally significant." He finds that initiation rites, whether into social maturity or cult membership, are particularly elaborate during this transitional stage of liminality. In his own words:

Case 14: Liminality.

"The transitional-being or "liminal persona" is defined by a name and by a set of symbols. The same name is very frequently employed to designate those who are being initiated into very different states of life.

For example, among the Ndembu of Zambia the name *mwadi* may mean various things: it may stand for "a boy novice in circumcision rites," or "a chief-designate undergoing his installation rites," or, yet again, "the first or ritual wife" who has important ritual duties in the domestic family. The symbolism attached to and surrounding the liminal persona is complex and bizarre. . . .

They are at once no longer classified and not yet classified. Insofar as they are no longer classified, the symbols that represent them are, in many societies, drawn from the biology of death, decomposition, catabolism, and other physical processes that have a negative tinge, such as menstruation. Thus, in some boys' initiations, newly circumcised boys are explicitly likened to menstruating women. Insofar as a neophyte is structurally "dead," he or she may be treated, for a long or short period, as a corpse is customarily treated. . . .

The neophyte may be buried, forced to lie motionless in the posture and direction of customary burial, may be stained black, or may be forced to live for a while in the company of masked and monstrous mummers representing the dead. . . .

The other aspect, that they are not yet classified, is often expressed in symbols modeled on processes of gestation and parturition. The neophytes are likened to or treated as embryos, newborn infants, or sucklings by symbolic means which vary from culture to culture.

The essential feature . . . is that the neophytes are neither living nor dead and both living and dead . . . their condition is one of ambiguity and paradox. . . . They have physical but not social reality, hence they have to be hidden . . . or disguised. . . ."[16]

The third phase, specified by van Gennep, is incorporation or aggregation. It is reentrance of a person or group back into

15. Arnold L. van Gennep, *The Rites of Passage,* (Chicago: University of Chicago Press, 1960).

16. Turner, "Betwixt and Between:" pp. 339-340.

society, this time with a new status. The theme for this phase tends to focus on symbolic rebirth of an individual.

Although these phases are claimed to be universal, the importance of each phase varies within rituals and between societies. We are aware that in fact they are not equally emphasized in all rites of passage within one society nor in similar rites of passage in all societies. Some societies emphasize the period of "separation," as in joining a convent, others elaborate on "liminality" as the Ndembu do in case 14. Joining the U. S. Army is a good example of a rite of passage which dramatizes both separation, when they kill the civilian in you, and liminality, when they isolate you in basic training centers. Still, others find "incorporation" as most important.

Turner finds this organization of ritual in terms of phases very useful and incorporates it in his own analyses, calling it "diachronic structure of ritual." He sees these phases as the processual dimension within ritual, but only as one part of his richly demonstrated framework of symbolic analysis.

Ritual As Symbolic Organization

Victor Turner explores the rituals of the East African Ndembu and gives us rich description with much detail. That in itself is a contribution. He does not, nor care to, deal with myth. This remained the exclusive property of structuralists. If I have to categorize Turner in terms of "schools" in anthropological theory I would say he is a psychological-structural-functional-symbolist, since he tries in fact to be all of that in one. Let us examine his framework more closely.

Turner spells out his goals and findings quite clearly. He distinguishes three levels of meaning: exegetical, operational, and positional. Exegetical meaning consists of the explanations received from the natives. He gets that from Ndembu etymology of the name of the symbolic object or act, and its observable characteristics. Operational meaning derives from a symbol's use, how and by whom it is obtained, set up, and manipulated in the rite. Finally, positional meaning derives from the relation of a symbol to other symbols either in one specific ritual or within a set of ritual symbols of the whole society.

To "penetrate the inner structure of ideas" contained in ritual, Turner begins with symbols, which are "the basic building-blocks or molecules" of ritual. Many of these symbols are characterized by the property of multivocality, "the fact that they possess many significations simultaneously." When all the symbols of a particular ritual are gathered we find that they are in the form of binary oppositions and as sets of pairs of opposed values (dyads) that lie along different planes in ritual space. For example, in the ritual Isoma the classificatory structure of dyads is schematically represented by Turner. See figure 4.4.

Looking down each of the three columns we find that certain symbols appear in more than one column. For example the opposition "Red Cock/White Pullet" in Isoma appears in all three columns. They are dominant symbols. The meaning of such a pair is derived from its association with other sets in the same column (plane). As Turner warns "equivalences may be sought within each column, not between them." It is precisely because of that positional meaning that symbols are multivocal. In our case "Red Cock/White Pullet" are associated with different sets of oppositions in each of the columns and therefore have different meanings. One reason for this is: "their nodal function . . . intersecting sets of classification."[17]

17. Victor Turner, "Planes of Classification in a Ritual of Life and Death," in *Reader in Comparative Religion*, pp. 153-166.

FIGURE 4.4
CLASSIFICATION OF DYADS IN ISOMA RITUAL

Longitudinal	Latitudinal	Altitudinal
Burrow/New Hole Grave/Fertility Death/Life Mystical Misfortune/Curing Hot Medicine/Cool Medicine Fire/Absence of Fire Blood/Water Red Cock/White Pullet	Left-Hand Fire/Right-Hand Fire Women/Men Patient/Patient's Husband Cultivated Roots/Bush Medicines White Pullet/Red Cock	Below Surface/Above Surface Candidates/Adepts Animals/Humans Naked/Clothed Medicine Roots/Medicine Leaves Shades/Living White Pullet/Red Cock

So What Is New?

Turner's use of exegetical meaning and operational meaning as levels of meaning is misleading. What these two technical terms mean is that his data are arrived at in two ways. One way is by asking the natives the labels for symbols and what these labels mean. Another way is by observing these symbols in action during rituals. Anthropologists have always been doing that in the field.

It is the positional meaning that is interesting. Symbols are seen by Ndembu natives in binary sets, and these sets derive their meaningfulness by being related to other sets that are in structural correspondence. For example, we find in figure 4-4 that the longitudinal plane includes: "Burrow/New Hole" which corresponds to "Grave/Fertility," to "Death/Life," etc. That is, the whole column is essentially a semantic environment for each set of symbols.

But Turner talks about dominant symbols. What makes a symbol dominant? Based on his analysis, a symbol's dominance or significance depends on the frequency of its recurrence in ritual(s). This is dominance in a statistical sense. "Red Cock/White Pullet" recurs in each of the three classificatory planes, so they are dominant.

Dominant symbols are multivocal. Said differently: a dyadic pair of symbols has several meanings because it is located in different semantic environments. Each dyad is "univocal" within its column, that is, within one semantic environment. But as these dyads appear in several classifications they serve as linking devices that give them the quality of multimeanings. This is a circular argument.

Whose Classification Is It?

Turner emphasizes the use of the vernacular when it comes to labeling of ritual phenomena as well as the etymology of the ritual symbols. The way the observable content is organized in "classificatory structure" is not in any systematic way elicited from the natives. He groups tangible and intangible elements in an order that is based on sensory qualities. This ordering is Turner's, not Ndembu. In other words, we have no emic nor ethnosemantic classification. But it is a useful attempt at ordering the chaotic content. It enabled Turner to locate "dominant symbols" because they reappeared in all columns, and clarified the notion of multivocality of symbols. Otherwise it provides no further enlightenment.

Native Classification

There is a long-standing anthropological tradition that focuses on the investigation of native categories and their relationships. It can be traced back to a classic notion formulated by Durkheim and Mauss.[18]

In the 1950s an influential approach to cultural structure emerged that builds on the assumption that the classification of things and events in a people's conceptual world will be mirrored in the semantic categories of their language.[19] That is, the way a people linguistically divide the world tells us what "things" they identify and what features they consider distinctive when they assign meaning to things. But that seems too dense. Let me give you an example relevant to your everyday life.

Case 15: "Have You Ever Heard of Lamb Steak?"

I am not an American native; nevertheless I have to go to American stores to buy meat. To request any specific cut I must understand the native categorization of meat. If, as ethnoscientists tell us, conceptual categories are reflected in linguistic distinctions, then a good way to start is to find out how meat and its parts are labeled. The American native meat classification was beginning to unfold. But I wondered if ordinary American people are aware (conscious) of that one very significant classification that they seem to deal with every day. I decided to experiment with that idea in my class on kinship.

I asked the students in class if they knew what "steak" was. There were puzzled faces and some deliberation.

Student: "Steak is a certain cut."
I: "What do you mean?"
Student: "It is a specific part of the animal."
I: "What part?"
Student: "The shoulder?"
I: "What animal?"
Student: "Any animal we eat."
I: "Have you heard of a lamb steak?"
Student: (silence) "We have lamb chops."
I: "But it is the same part of the animal."
Student: "Steak is big."
I: "Have you heard of pork steak?"
Student: "No. I know, steak has a bone in it."
I: "And lamb chop does not?"
Student: *"But steak is more meat; it is big and juicy."*

Finally we all agreed. Steak should be beef. Beef must be highly valued by Americans. In fact I recall when Rick Adams had just returned from Argentina to Texas and I said: "You look great; did you enjoy it there?" He answered, as only a real American would, "Tremendously. We ate beef every day."

So beef is a big thing. It has to be singled out in the classification of meats. Steak is a label that reflects the differentiation that Americans (along with other Westerners) make, and tells us what kind of meat is most highly valued.

By finding out how a people cut up their own world and what features are distinctive, we can avoid superimposing our preconceptions and cultural biases on other people's conceptual systems. Toward that goal, the ethnoscientists assumed that linguistic methods and models will be appropriate to

18. Émile Durkheim and Marcel Mauss, *Primitive Classification,* trans. R. Needham (Chicago: University of Chicago Press, 1963).

19. Stephen A. Tyler, ed., *Cognitive Anthropology* (New York: Holt, Rinehart, and Winston, 1969), pp. 1-5.

other cultural realms. So they devised systematic eliciting techniques modeled on those in linguistics aiming at more rigor than the usual style of fieldwork permits.

Charles O. Frake and others attempted to map the structure of subsystems of folk classification with sophistication and rigor. Frake, who explored the way the Subanun of the Philippines diagnose skin diseases, extended this procedure to other areas of Subanun life, including religious behavior. And the "new ethnography" also entered the superhuman domain as viewed by humans.

Keesing and Keesing sum up the value of ethnoscience very nicely by saying:

"[They] hope to transcend the artificiality of a 'chapter title' approach to a people's culture. 'Economics,' 'political structure,' and ['religion'] are misleading but convenient organizing devices. But if we hope to describe the structure of a people's own conceptual world, they are worse than misleading. We want to find out what realms people divide their world into, not force it into our predevised compartments. Their systems might turn out to correspond in some respects to 'chapter title' comparative frameworks. But that is something we would have to discover about another people's conceptual world; we cannot use a method that assumes it."[20]

This whole orientation raises several questions. Once we have discovered the ordering of a people's conceptual world, where do we go from there? Can we go beyond "mapping . . . limited and neatly bounded semantic domains" such as Tzeltal firewood, Subanun diseases, Tenejapa ladino weddings, etc.?[21] As Keesing puts it, "the messianic optimism . . . has yielded so few fragments of cultural description."[22] As anthropologists become more knowledgeable about cultures and more sophisticated in techniques, we are struck by the complexity of human systems that makes them less easily amenable to formal ethnography as anticipated. On the other hand, we cannot deny nor ignore the precision in ethnodescription. Perhaps we should extend the technique to closer (look at Spradley's work) and more practical everyday problems. As was suggested in a recent conversation, "if we can tell the ordinary, eligible American precisely how to get his monthly social security check, we can contribute to relevance and sanity."

It would be more useful in general, however, if we look at ethnoscience as ethnosemantic discovery procedures and use them as techniques (supplemented by other discovery procedures) to discover aspects of the native's own universe. For us to go beyond precise description to reach the level of explanation we will need to shift our attention from discovery procedures to theory.[23] We also have to move away from uniqueness of cultures (as we seem to have done in the last several years) to search for universal structures. It is only in the context of broader theory that uniqueness of cultural systems is significant. This is precisely where Lévi-Straussian work is progressive. Turner misses the significance and generality of structural work interested in

20. Roger M. Keesing and Felix M. Keesing, *New Perspectives in Cultural Anthropology* (New York: Holt, Rinehart, and Winston, 1971), p. 320.

21. Duane G. Metzger and Gerald E. Williams, "Some Procedures and Results in the Study of Native Categories: Tzeltal 'Firewood,'" *American Anthropologist* 68, no. 2 (1966):389-407; C. O. Frake, "The Diagnosis of Disease among the Subanun of Mindanao," *American Anthropologist* 63 (1961):113-132; Duane G. Metzger and Gerald E. Williams, "A Formal Ethnographic Analysis of Tenejapa Ladino Weddings," *American Anthropologist* 65 (1963):1076-1101.

22. Roger Keesing, "Theories of Culture," in *Annual Review of Anthropology*, vol. 3, eds. B. J. Siegel, A. R. Beals, and S. A. Tyler (Palo Alto, Calif.: Annual Reviews, 1974), pp. 73-97.

23. Emmon Bach, *Syntactic Theory* (New York: Holt, Rinehart, and Winston, 1974), pp. 15-18.

the mind when he compares his own contribution based on Ndembu analyses saying that "the whole person, *not just the mind*, is . . . involved in the life or death issues" of rituals.[24] Turner exemplifies a school of thought that finds the universal significance of ritual in its emotive and sensory aspects rather than in logical ones.

Function And Emotions In Ritual

After demonstrating the richness in meaning of Ndembu ritual symbols, Turner tells us that these symbols and their relations are "evocative devices for rousing, channeling, and domesticating powerful emotions, such as hate, fear, affection, and grief."[25] A major function of ritual is to channel emotion into the norms of society and make what is obligatory also desirable.

This claim is reminiscent of rituals as viewed by Durkheim and Radcliffe-Brown, who focused on collective sentiment and social integration, and Malinowski, who was concerned with individual psychology and needs. At one point an issue over whether anxiety caused ritual or vice versa became very heated between Radcliffe-Brown and Malinowski in the 1930s.

Do We Have Ritual Because We're Anxious or Are We Anxious from Ritual?

Malinowski says that in order to understand phenomena such as the function of ritual we have to look to individual psychology. Whenever humans are faced with situations that are beyond their powers of practical control or are confronted with problems that are beyond their knowledge, they become helpless and go through feelings of fear and anxiety. Because of a real physiological need they resort to ritual activities.

On the contrary, argues Radcliffe-Brown, humans are more likely to experience concern and anxiety when a customary ritual is not performed than they are to turn to ritual procedures when they feel anxious. In refuting Malinowski's anxiety hypothesis, Radcliffe-Brown draws on his Andamanese material. Were it not for the existence of the rite, the individual would feel no anxiety.

For example, in Andamanese childbirth situations the woman feels anxious because she was told that delivery is a dangerous, painful experience that must be safeguarded by ritual. So certain rites efficacious in warding off childbirth danger are performed, and anxiety is thus relieved. It is not individual sentiment that we are talking about but societal expectation.

In other words, whereas Malinowski claims that anxiety gives rise to ritual, Radcliffe-Brown rejects the notion that individual anxiety gives rise to social expression. Society expects an individual to feel anxiety on certain occasions.

It appears then that Andaman parents do not feel anxiety at the fact of childbirth, but only when the ritual of childbirth is not performed properly. Their techniques allow them to manipulate and control natural forces fully. When they do everything possible and perform the rituals properly, they display little overt anxiety. But when the rites are not properly performed, anxiety results.

George Homans attempts to resolve the impasse. He finds the two positions to be complementary rather than contradictory. He proposes the notions of "primary" and "secondary" anxieties and rituals. Applying these notions, he says that Malinowski is discussing initial anxiety situation, that ritual dispels anxiety but, he claims, anxiety remains latent. Radcliffe-Brown's theory supplements this, since there is secondary ritual that relieves the anxiety that was dis-

24. Turner, "Planes of Classification," p. 166.
25. Ibid.

placed from the original situation. The secondary ritual has the function of dispelling the secondary anxiety arising from the breach of ritual.[26]

It is this kind of argument at this level that makes Lévi-Strauss feel pessimistic about the prospects for a scientific study of religion. His view cannot be more clearly phrased than in his own words:

"Psychological interpretations were withdrawn from the intellectual field only to be introduced again in the field of affectivity, thus adding to the inherent defects of the psychological school the mistake of deriving clear-cut ideas from vague emotions. Instead of trying to enlarge the framework of our logic to include processes which, whatever their apparent differences, belong to the same kind of intellectual operation, a naive attempt was made to reduce them to inarticulate emotional drives, which resulted only in hampering our studies."[27]

Furthermore, Leach points out that a distinction between information expressed in verbal form, such as myth, and information expressed in nonverbal action, such as ritual, is false. This reminds us of Keesing's point mentioned earlier about the "chapter title" approach to cultural systems that divides them into law, economics, kinship, and religion. My own work on Zapotec beliefs and rituals supports a systemic approach that transcends boundaries of that kind. These distinctions are not very productive. They neither describe adequately nor explain. In the next and final chapter I will demonstrate how myths and rituals are better seen in the context of belief systems organized in terms of concept, structure, and meaning.

For Further Reading

Frake, Charles O. "A Structural Description of Subanun 'Religious Behavior.' " in *Explorations in Honor of George Peter Murdock,* ed. W. A. Goodenough. New York: McGraw-Hill Book Co., 1964. This paper emphasizes ethnographic methodology and tries to answer the question "How does the field worker *recognize* 'religious behavior'?" by spelling out the procedure for labeling activities using native terms for them. He ends up with the discovery that what we would label "religion" is for the Subanun, a collection of techniques for getting things done.

Fromkin, V. and R. Rodman. *An Introduction to Language*. New York: Holt, Rinehart, and Winston, 1974. A general introductory book written from the modern transformational viewpoint but which contains wide coverage of linguistics and related areas. Charming use of anecdotes and comic strips as illustrations.

Leach, Edmund. *Claude Lévi-Strauss.* New York: The Viking Press, 1970. An explanation of Lévi-Strauss's ideas about human universals, symbols, mythical thinking, and kinship. Leach briefly relates these ideas to the intellectual movements that influenced them. A good introduction to Lévi-Strauss's work.

Lévi-Strauss, Claude. "The Story of Asdiwal." in *The Structural Study of Myth and Totemism,* ed. E. Leach. London: Tavistock Publications, 1967. An examination of a Pacific coast myth to discover how its events are organized from the standpoints of geography, technology and economics, society, and cosmology. This makes it possible to find the underlying logical structure common to all of these, and then to relate this myth to variants of it from nearby territories.

Lyons, John. *Noam Chomsky.* New York: The Viking Press, 1970. A basic introduction to Chomsky's work, covering his linguistic theory and the philosophical and psychologi-

26. George C. Hommans, "Anxiety and Ritual: the Theories of Malinowski and Radcliffe-Brown," in *Reader in Comparative Religion,* pp. 83-88.

27. Claude Lévi-Strauss, "The Structural Study of Myth," in *Reader in Comparative Religion,* p. 207.

cal implications of this viewpoint. Better read in its entirety without getting too hung up on details.

Turner, Victor. *The Forest of Symbols.* Ithaca: Cornell University Press, 1967. A very detailed description of ritual and ritual objects in an African culture. Symbolic objects are viewed as tangible devices for tying ethical concepts to the emotions. Read one or two articles completely to understand his position, and skim the rest.

Bibliography

Bach, Emmon. 1974. *Syntactic Theory.* New York: Holt, Rinehart, and Winston.

Bascom, William. 1965. "The Forms of Folklore." *The Journal of American Folklore* 78:3-20.

Boas, Franz. 1938. *The Mind of Primitive Man.* New York: The Macmillan Co.

Chomsky, Noam and Halle, Morris. 1968. *The Sound Pattern of English.* New York: Harper & Row.

Durkheim, Émile and Mauss, Marcel. 1963. *Primitive Classification.* Translated by R. Needham. Chicago: University of Chicago Press.

El Guindi, Fadwa. 1966. "Ritual and the River in Dahmit." In *Contemporary Egyptian Nubia.* New Haven, Conn.: Human Relations Area Files Press. Edited by R. Fernea, pp. 239-256.

Fernea, Robert, ed. 1966. *Contemporary Egyptian Nubia.* New Haven, Conn.: Human Relations Area Files Press.

Frake, C. O. 1961. "The Diagnosis of Disease among the Subanun of Mindanao." *American Anthropologist* 63:113-132.

Gluckman, Max. 1965. *Politics, Law and Ritual in Tribal Society.* Chicago: Aldine Publishing Co.

Homans, George C. "Anxiety and Ritual: the Theories of Malinowski and Radcliffe-Brown." In *Reader in Comparative Religion.* Edited by W. A. Lessa and E. Z. Vogt, 3rd ed. New York: Harper & Row.

Jakobson, Roman and Halle, Morris. 1956. *Fundamentals of Language.* The Hague: Mouton & Co.

Keesing, Roger. 1974. "Theories of Culture." In *Annual Review of Anthropology.* Edited by B. J. Siegel, A. Beals, and S. Tyler, vol. 3. Palo Alto, Cal.: Annual Reviews.

Keesing, Roger M. and Keesing, Felix M. 1971. *New Perspectives in Cultural Anthropology.* New York: Holt, Rinehart, and Winston.

Lessa, William A. 1972. "Discoverer-of-the-Sun." In *Reader in Comparative Religion.* Edited by W. A. Lessa and E. Z. Vogt, 3rd ed. New York: Harper & Row.

Lessa, William A. and Vogt, Evon Z., eds. 1972. *Reader in Comparative Religion.* 3rd ed. New York: Harper & Row.

Lévi-Strauss, Claude. 1963. *Structural Anthropology.* New York: Basic Books.

Malinowski, Bronislaw. 1926. *Myth in Primitive Psychology.* New York: W. W. Norton & Co.

Metzger, Duane G. and Williams, Gerald E. 1963. "A Formal Ethnographic Analysis of Tenejapa Ladino Weddings." *American Anthropologist* 65:1076-1101.

———. 1966. "Some Procedures and Results in the Study of Native Categories: Tzeltal 'Firewood.' " *American Anthropologist* 68:389-407.

Siegel, B. J.; Beals, A. R.; and Tyler, S. A., eds. 1974. *Annual Review of Anthropology.* vol. 3. Palo Alto, Cal.: Annual Reviews.

Trubetzkoy, N. S. 1969 *Principles of Phonology.* (Translation of *Gründzuge der Phonologie.* 1939. Travaux du Cercle Linguistique de Prague 7). Berkeley: University of California Press.

Turner, Victor. 1972. "Betwixt and Between: the Liminal Period in *Rites de Passage.*" In *Reader in Comparative Religion.* Edited by W. A. Lessa and E. Z. Vogt, 3rd ed. New York: Harper & Row.

———. 1972. "Planes of Classification in a Ritual of Life and Death." In *Reader in Compara-*

tive Religion. Edited by W. A. Lessa and E. Z. Vogt, 3rd ed. New York: Harper & Row.

Tyler, Stephen A., ed. 1969. *Cognitive Anthropology.* New York: Holt, Rinehart, and Winston.

Van Gennep, Arnold L. 1960. *The Rites of Passage.* (Translation of *Les Rites de Passage.* 1909. Paris.) Chicago: University of Chicago Press.

5 Belief Systems: Concept, Structure, and Meaning

In this chapter I will demonstrate how Zapotec ritual has "structure." Because any discussion about structure "seems" too difficult for students to understand, I will make my discussion in this chapter somewhat more personal than in the previous chapters. I will talk about my data, where and how I collected it, the background of my orientation, how I became interested in that particular problem, and how structure began to emerge in my analysis. In this chapter I hope:

(1) to demonstrate that ritual has structure;

(2) to suggest an alternative way of looking at religion; and

(3) to show that structural theory is very promising and that we do not have to be graduate students to begin to grasp its principles.

I TAKE MALINOWSKI IN ONE HAND AND LÉVI-STRAUSS IN THE OTHER WHEN I GO TO THE FIELD

The data in this analysis was collected in a Zapotec farming community of approximately 900 people situated nine miles ESE of Oaxaca City, Mexico. I was stationed in that community in the summer of 1967 through the Stanford Field School and continue to do research there. I received my Ph.D. training in Texas. But before graduate school I was in Egypt, where I was engaged in doing research in urban Egypt, rural Egypt, and, more importantly for me, in Nubia for five years.

From my experience in Egypt I learned the Malinowskianism so important in my field approach: detailed collection of data with equal emphasis on observation and interviewing. From my training in Texas and Oaxaca I learned the value of constructing abstract models to achieve precision and rigor in description, and, when possible, adequate explanation. In other words, when I went to the field in Oaxaca (1970-1971) I took Malinowski in one hand and Lévi-Strauss in the other and proceeded to do my research.

HOW I CAME UPON THE PROBLEM

In my Zapotec community I began my fieldwork by observing what was happening around me and attending as many activities as possible. Until a child died. The ritual for his death was called *angelito,* and it took three days of events and activities.

The outstanding feature of this ritual was that it was a very joyful, happy event. People were dancing to lively music and drinking mescal and seemed happy. This attitude of joyfulness puzzled me. Common sense says that people are not happy when their child has died. I saw a paradox of happiness in death. I got interested in death.

I JUST HAD TO MOVE FROM DEATH TO MARRIAGE

I checked the literature on Middle America and found a distinction made between death of child (*angelito*) and death of adult (*difunto*), which appeared to correspond with the distinction made in my Zapotec community.

I continued to attend more deaths of each kind. Gradually I was able to uncover the features that characterized the two death rituals. Such aspects as the ringing of churchbells announcing the death, the type of music played by the local band, the offers given in each ritual, the corpse and coffin preparation, the funeral procession, the burial activities, and the categories of people participating in various parts and days of the ritual are summarized in figure 5-1 in the form of a set of binary oppositions.[1]

Then a 21-year-old young man died. Would he be given an *angelito* ritual or a *difunto* ritual? I wondered. To my surprise, he was given an *angelito* ritual. I asked why. I was told that this was because he is *angelito*. I asked: "Do you consider X a child?" "No, he is a young man." "Then why is he not a *difunto*?" "Because he is not a *pecador* (sinful person)." "What is he?" "*Inocente*

1. Fadwa El Guindi, "The Internal Structure of the Zapotec Conceptual System," *Journal of Symbolic Anthropology* 1 (1973):18.

FIGURE 5.1
BINARY FORMS OF DEATH

Aspects of Ritual Activity	*Angelito*	*Difunto*
Church Bells	Fast Lively	Slow Sad
Music	Happy Dancing Music	Sad Funeral Marches
Coffin	White	Black (or Dark Blue)
Procession (From House to Cemetery)	Happy Nonstop Fast	Sad 3 stops Slow
Offerings	*Cariño* (Soda+Mescal)	*Responso* (Money)
Sex Distinction in Clothing the Corpse, Burial, and Grave Location, etc.	Absent	Present
People	The Significant Category is *Invitados* (the Invited)	The Significant Category is *voluntarios* (Volunteers)
Sequencing of Events	3-4 Days	10-11 Days

(innocent). He is innocent." Certainly this 21-year-old who spent every weekend in Oaxaca City was not that innocent. Not the way I understood innocent to be. I asked the people: "What makes him innocent?" "He is not married." So that was it. Marriage was the criterion which distinguished *angelito* from *difunto,* not age. That is, *angelito* is "death of not-married," while *difunto* is "death of married."

RITUAL AS SETS OF CATEGORIES

Therefore we see that I started with *angelito,* moved to its relationship to *difunto,* the two being the differentiated categories within "death," and moved from "death" to "marriage" because of the way they are related to each other. I was unable to deal with individual ritual activities as independent isolated entities; the data forced me to look at them as sets of categories related in specific form.

DEATH IS HAPPY BECAUSE DEATH IS STRONG

This is meant in a structural sense of course. What I am saying is that we can see that there is a "relationship" existing between death and marriage which cannot be discerned at the level of content alone. I will briefly discuss the nature of this relationship in terms of three aspects: internal differentiation; sociological categorization; and affect.

Internal Differentiation

Death is characterized by a relatively greater internal differentiation than marriage. For example, through death one is categorized either as "people" and buried in the "new cemetery" or "nonpeople" and buried in the "old cemetery." People are those who have died a natural death as opposed to those who died unbaptized, murdered, in an accident, or through suicide. Those who have died a natural death are either *difuntos* (death of married) or *angelitos* (death of not-married). This is diagrammed below.

Sociological Categorization

A similar kind of differentiation is seen on the level of kinship relations. The sociological world, as exemplified in the categories of people in the Zapotec ritual of death, is divided into the permanent adult members of the household who become *caseros* (people of the house who "*manda,*" command) as opposed to all the other groups of people who are involved in the same ritual. Permanent members of the household who are not

FIGURE 5.2
INTERNAL DIFFERENTIATION OF DEATH

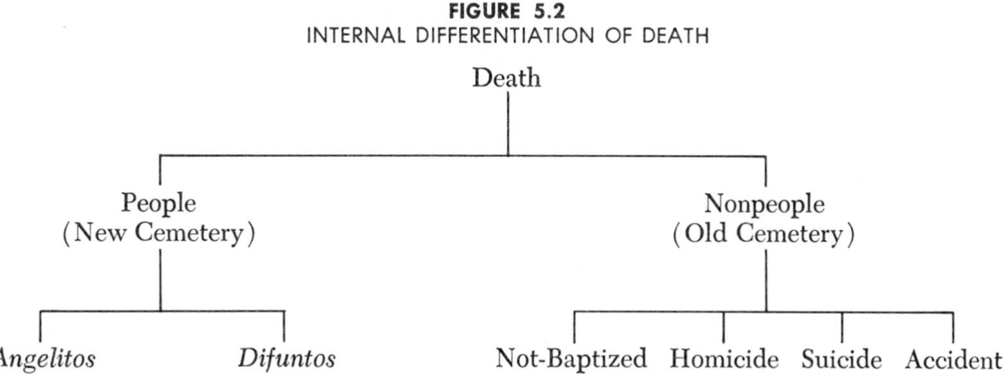

adult are potential *caseros*. They do not yet command.

Non*caseros* may be *voluntarios* or *invitados*. *Voluntarios* are related to the *caseros* consanguineally, fictively, affinally, or through ties of friendship, neighborship, or through obligations of *guelaguetza* (institutionalized form of lending and borrowing of items such as money, turkeys, tortillas, etc.). *Voluntarios* may either explicitly volunteer their services to the *caseros*, or merely fulfill any services the *caseros* request from them.

Invitados may be consanguineal, affinal, or fictive kin who are invited by the *caseros* to attend part or all of the ritual activity. Accepting the invitation implies the acceptance of certain obligations to be fulfilled toward the *caseros* in the form of services in the house where the ritual is taking place, or errands anywhere in the community (occasionally outside the community).

Mediating the categories *caseros* and non*caseros* are the ritual officials. These are the *rezadores* (prayer men) and their assistants, the *sacristán* (sacristan) and the *acólitos* (acolytes), the *panteoneros* (graveyard caretakers), and the *música* (musical band).

It is the *voluntarios* and *invitados* who give gifts, offers of money, mescal and cigarettes, flowers, or candles to the *caseros*. Ritual officials do not offer anything other than the services defined by the position they occupy in the community.

Both non*caseros* and ritual officials are served food and drink, mescal, and cigarettes. The ritual meal consists of a drink of hot chocolate with bread, and *mole* with meat (beef or turkey) and tortilla (occassionally *mole* is substituted by beef stew or beans). People are obligated to drink mescal and accept (not necessarily smoke) cigarettes throughout their stay in the house. They are also obligated to finish all the food and drink served them or else carry the remaining food back home when they leave.

Only the *casero* himself could release anybody from his obligation. He is in command (*manda*) all during the ritual and sees to it that all jobs and errands are done and problems avoided or resolved. His right to *manda* extends to all those who are under the obligation of "participating" due to their relationship with him, whether they do actually attend or not.

In one instance that I observed, for example, my informant was standing in the street in the village watching a funeral procession go by. The *casero* called out asking him to do a ritual-related errand. Abel had to do it despite the fact that he did not otherwise participate in the death ritual nor attend it at all. But the deceased is related to Abel. The obligation stands and the *casero* has the full right to enforce it. For clarification the categories of people in ritual are diagrammed in figure 5-3.

Moreover, in association with death we find a relatively greater degree of ritual of a more complex kind. This complexity is represented in figure 5-4 in terms of the categorized sequential activities and the various categories of people in each activity. Conversely, marriage shows a low degree of complexity in the ritual and sociological organization, along with a relatively low degree of internal differentiation—there is only one kind of marriage ritual: *fandango,* which is a one-day set of activities. And there is only one undifferentiated sociological world conceptually conceived: *invitados.*

Affect

On the attitudinal level we find that death is associated with a strong attitude. In *angelitos* (death ritual of not-married) there is much joyful positive affect; and in *difuntos* (death ritual of married) there is

FIGURE 5.3
CATEGORIES OF PEOPLE IN DEATH RITUAL

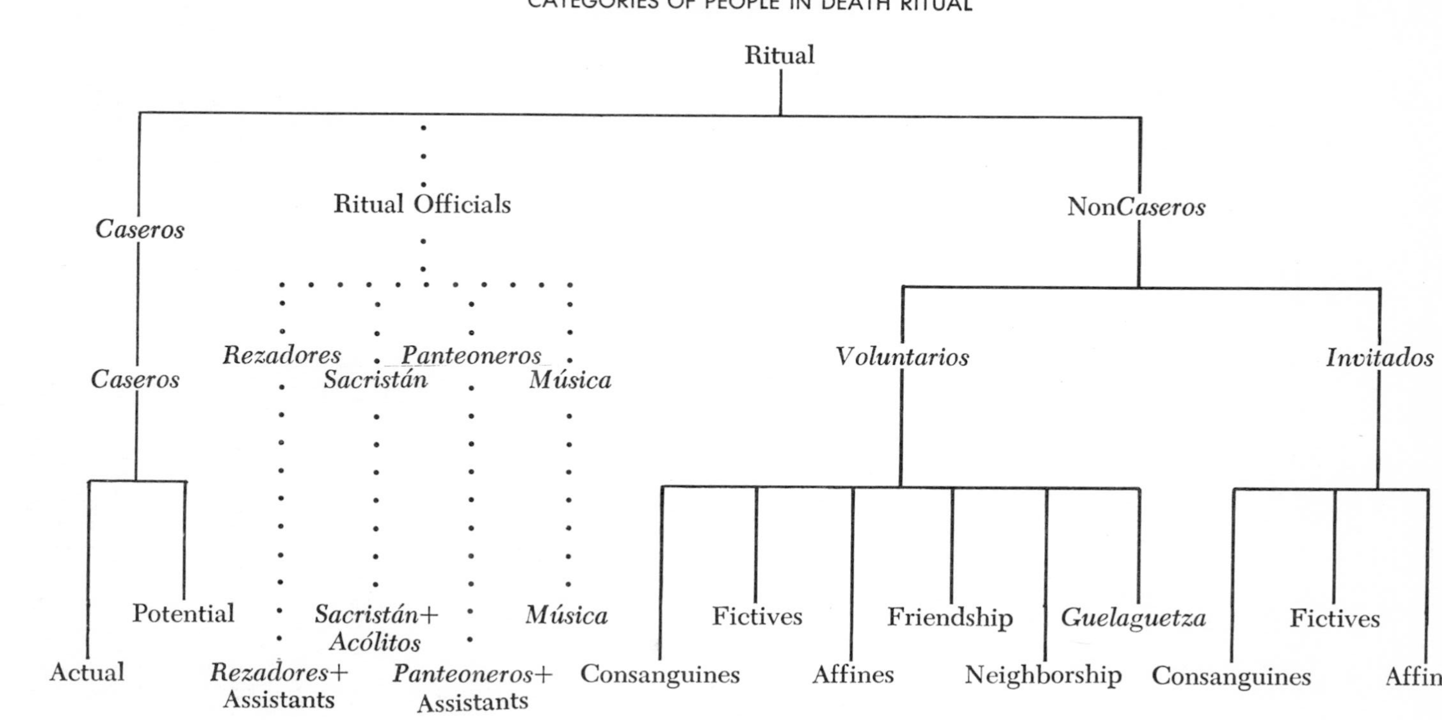

FIGURE 5.4

COMPLEX CATEGORIZATION OF DAYS AND PEOPLE IN DEATH

	Angelito	*Difunto*
Velorio (Day of Candles)	*Vol.* + *Inv.* + RO_1	*Vol.* + RO_1
Entierro (Day of Burial)	*Vol.* + *Inv.* + RO_2 + RO_3 + RO_4	*Vol.* + RO_2 + RO_3 + RO_4
Botella (Day of bottle—one or two days)	*Vol.* + *Inv.*	*Vol.*
Reso de Cruz (Prayer of Cross)		*Vol.* + RO_1
Levantar la Cruz (Raising the Cross)		*Inv.* + RO_1 + RO_3
Botella de Cruz (Bottle of Cross—One or Two Days)		*Vol.*

Vol. = *Voluntarios* (Volunteers)
Inv. = *Invitados* (Invited)
RO = Ritual Officials

[1]*Rezadores* + Assistants
[2]*Sacristán* + *Acólitos*
[3]*Panteoneros*
[4]*Música*

very sad negative affect. Both attitudes are strongly and clearly expressed: one is very happy; the other is very sad. There is no doubt whatsoever about affect associated with each kind of death ritual. On the other hand, if we look at marriage, we find that its ritual, *fandango,* is very businesslike; all people involved are concerned about doing the "proper thing" without expressing any emotive behavior, whether positive or negative. The wedding ritual just goes on. Even dancing just goes on. They are very busy sitting properly in the correct places, eating properly in the correct fashion, distributing food properly, dancing with the right people, and so on. There is little or no affect with marriage.

If we then look at death and marriage as conceptual categories, we could say that we find affective dispositions associated with the different concepts. Death evokes either much joyful positive affect in *angelitos* or very sad negative affect in *difuntos,* while marriage evokes weak or no affect.

To recapitulate: I considered death versus marriage in terms of three aspects. Internal differentiation is high in death, low in marriage; sociological categorization is complex in death, simple in marriage; affect is strong (positive/negative) in death, weak (neutral) in marriage. This can be represented in diagram form. See figure 5-5.

Therefore, instead of regarding death as an isolated phenomenon, this analysis has focused on relations between sets of phenomena. By understanding the nature of the relationship between conceptual categories —death and marriage in this case—what appears to be a paradoxical attitude, such as "happiness in death," can be resolved. How? This still seems to be contrary to common sense which says that death, being termination of life, is a sad event. Yet happiness is characteristic of death (of not-married) in

FIGURE 5.5
DEATH IS STRONG, MARRIAGE IS WEAK

	Death	Marriage
Internal Differentiation	High	Low
Sociological Categorization	Complex	Simple
Affect	Positive/Negative	Neutral

Zapotec culture. Moreover, it is consistently and consciously rationalized by the people in their statements and activities.

It may begin to make more sense if we look at this paradoxical happiness in death in terms of its logical relationship within the set of positive and negative attitudes. As I have demonstrated, death is differentiated into a binary opposition of *angelito* and *difunto,* the former associated with a strong positive affect (happiness), and the latter with a strong negative affect (sadness), while marriage evokes little or no affect. Therefore death (of not-married) is happy because death is strong.

FIGURE 5.6

MARRIAGE MEDIATES DEATH

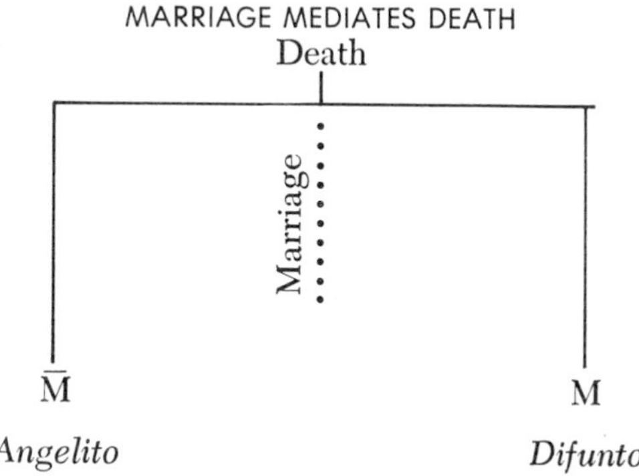

WITHOUT MARRIAGE DEATH CANNOT EXIST

We have seen how death is differentiated into two categories based on marriage. Marriage, in that sense, creates the distinction between *angelito* (death of not-married) and *difunto* (death of married). Marriage, then, can be said to mediate the concept of death. In this particular conceptual environment it is mediating in the sense of operating as a defining, differentiating category. It brings about the differentiation within "death." Without marriage "death" cannot exist.

POWER IN RITUAL AND EMERGING STRUCTURE

I then moved from death to other ritual activities. As I observed more rituals I noticed that people who in ordinary everyday activities are identified as Natalia, José, Martin, disappeared in ritual. Personalities are eliminated. Instead categories of people become basic. There is an element of substitutability that becomes important in ritual.

For example in death ritual: all people of "house," who are otherwise known as Apolinar and Natalia become *caseros* as opposed to all the rest of the people who are involved in that same ritual. So that in death ritual two basic categories are created, *caseros* versus non*caseros.* If we go back to figure 5-3 we see how these two are further differentiated, such that all the categories of people involved in the death ritual are represented. Mediating the opposition—*caseros* versus non*caseros*—is the category "ritual officials."

But let us dwell on this opposition, *caseros* versus non-*caseros.* What defines the sociological category *caseros?* Authority. *Caseros* command (*mandan*). Those people of the house who are adult, are in command throughout the ritual and see that jobs and errands are done, problems are avoided or resolved. Some form begins to unfold in terms of the sociological world in ritual.

I proceeded to examine other rituals. For example, the ritual of "change of church committee" (*Cambio de Comité del Templo*) is an annual political ritual that takes place in church. Naturally I looked for the category *caseros* which is one category within the oppositional set that characterized the sociological world in death. I could not find it.

Instead, I found that the *cambio* is characterized by a different set of categories: *autoridad* (municipal officers) versus *comité* (committee), and a mediating category.[2]

Similarly, in wedding ritual the basic sociological opposition is: *huehuete* (old man, ritual leader) versus *invitados,* and a mediating category.[3] Ritual of *Todos Santos* (All Saints) involves still another opposition: *caseros* versus "living kin," and a mediating category.[4]

In other words, if we look at the content of these categories:

death = *caseros* / non*caseros,*
and mediating category;
cambio = *autoridad* / *comité,*
and mediating category;
wedding = *huehuete* / *invitados*
and mediating category;
Todos Santos = *caseros* / living kin,
and mediating category;

we find that it does vary from one ritual to the other. But if we look at the form of the relationship between these categories, we immediately see that it is invariant. All the ritual activities which I have examined in the Zapotec system are characterized by a sociological world divided into those who are in command (power), e.g., *caseros, autoridad,* huehuete, etc., versus those who are obligated to participate and are not in command (nonpower), e.g., non*caseros, comité, invitados,* etc. This can be represented as follows:

R

P   P

where P stands for power category and P for nonpower category. This opposition P/P is related by a mediating category:

R

P   M   P

This forms the ritual base, which means that all ritual activities in the Zapotec system share this base, and it follows that all Zapotec rituals are variants. Different variants, such as *angelito,* wedding, *Todos Santos, etc.,* are generated from the base.

CONCEPTUAL STRUCTURE

The category *casero* not only led me to a more abstract level of structural properties which differentiates the sociological world in ritual, it also led me to examine the natives' notion of *casa* (house). *Caseros* (people of house) derives from *casa* (house). House was discussed at length in case 11 chapter 3. But here let me relate a Zapotec myth which tells us much about the structural position of house in the natives' spatial domain.

Case 16: The Bruja Myth.

"There was a *bruja* (witch) who lived in a house with her husband. They had a child.

2. Fadwa El Guindi, "The Structural Correlates of Power in Ritual," in *Anthropology of Power,* eds. R. N. Adams and R. Fogelson (New York: Academic Press, in press).

3. Fadwa El Guindi, "Internal Constraints on Structure," in *New Trends in Structural Anthropology,* ed. Ino Rossi (forthcoming).

4. Fadwa El Guindi, "Structure and Natives' Knowledge of Culture," in *Toward the Sociology of Symbolic Structures,* ed. Ino Rossi (forthcoming).

pesadas) the bruja goes out roaming around the village on her mission. She kidnaps children, takes them to the field and plays with them. The *bruja* throws the child back and forth like a ball. The *bruja* is always two. After exhausting the child with play, she carries him back home and puts him back in the mother's arms. When the *bruja* takes a child from the mother's arm she puts a grindstone pestle (*mano del metate*) in the mother's arms instead of the child. This way the mother would not miss the child thinking it is her child in her arms. Mothers always embrace their babies while they are asleep. The *bruja* knows that.

In the morning the mother finds the child very sick and then the child dies. She finds blue marks all over the child's body, and this way she knows that the *bruja* killed him. Nothing can cure a child who is sick from the *bruja*.

The *bruja's* neighbor was watching the *bruja* all this time and she knew that she is a *bruja*. One day the neighbor went to the *bruja's* husband and warned him. She told him that his wife is a *bruja* and that he should be careful because the *bruja* will also kill her own child. When the *bruja* does not find any child to play with she kills her own child.

One day the *bruja* left the house and went around the village on her mission looking for a child. She went from house to house. There were no children. All the mothers that day were holding their babies in their arms. So the *bruja* could not kidnap any baby to play with in the field.

The *bruja* returned home at the end of the day. The husband was already in bed and had their child in his arms. The *bruja* went close to the child. At this moment the husband looked up at her and asked what she was doing. She said that she was getting ready to go to bed. After a while the *bruja* tried to pull the child away from the father. But the child was tied to the father by the arms and waist. She began to untie the child. She held the child and at this moment the husband heard a buzzard on top of the house roof. He knew for sure that she is a *bruja*. She was trying to kidnap their own child. But just when the *bruja* was about to take off with the child she found that the child was also tied by the ankles to the father. The father had tied his child to him in order to find out whether his wife is really a *bruja* or not. It was too late, and she had gone out of the house already, and the child was left safely behind because he was tied.

The husband got up quickly, untied the child, and took the child to the neighbor. He told her that now he knows that she is right. His wife is a *bruja*, and she tried to kidnap their own child. He left the child with the neighbor and went out to follow the *bruja* to see where she goes.

The *bruja* went to the cemetery. Just in front of the *ermita* (cemetery shrine) he saw many heads. The *brujas* leave their heads there in front of the *ermita* and then go to the field to do their evil. So the *bruja* left her head in front of the *ermita*, changed into a buzzard, and flew away. The husband immediately switched heads. He switched his wife's head with a male head that was there.

Then the *bruja* returned to the cemetery, to put her head back on. After she put her head on she realized that it is a male's head. It had a beard and a mustache. She covered her face with her *rebozo* (head shawl) and went home.

At home she kept her face covered. When she talked to her husband her voice was a man's voice. She couldn't remove the *rebozo* or reveal her male head. Eventually she died from *verguenza* (shame)."

House/Field and Cemetery

There are several interesting aspects in the preceding body of data: the Bruja Myth. But I will confine the analysis at this point to the boundaries of the Zapotec spatial universe. We find that the three concepts, house, cemetery, and field, represent three boundary points. The witch goes from house to field and from field to house. However, it does not go directly; it has to go from house to cemetery to field, and after doing its "evil" in the field it again goes to the cemetery before returning to the house. So just in terms of their spatial positions we can see house/field as a contrast pair linked by cemetery. But we need to know more about these concepts.

Based on native statements, observed behavior, and observed ritual activities the two concepts, house and field, emerge as a conceptual set defined as a set of binary oppositions. This is summarized in figure 5-7 below.

FIGURE 5.7
HOUSE AND FIELD AS A
SET OF BINARY CATEGORIES

House	Field
Inside	Outside
Has Boundary	Has No Boundary
Confidence	Distrust
Good	Evil
Sacred	Not-Sacred
No Danger	Danger
Edible Food	Not-Edible Food
Blessed Water	Not-Blessed Water
Licit Sex	Illicit Sex
Body + Soul	*Tono* (animal part of person)
Jesus + Saints	Devil + *Matlazigua* (Vicious Supernatural Being Threatening to Maleness of Men)
Ritual	Not-Ritual

We find, then, that the concepts of house and field make up a set characterized by a positive instead of a negative relationship. As a contrast set it is very clearly defined, and each of the two concepts is marked by a rigid categorical boundary on the ideological level. Natives have no doubt whatsoever about the meaning of each of these concepts; there is no ambiguity associated with this oppositional set.

Conversely, the concept, cemetery, is associated with a loosely defined ideology and paradoxical attitude. For example, when I asked the natives about cemetery-related activities I was given contradictory answers. In terms of grave location, to give specific instances, I was told that burying people is based on a north/south division of the cemetery based on sex alone. Irrespective of age and marital status women were buried on one side and men on the other. Other informants found such information to be ridiculous and stated that burial is in terms of different criteria. Primarily the division is based on whether the dead is *angelito* or *difunto. Angelitos* are buried in the center (east/west axis), while *difuntos* are buried on both sides of the *angelitos,* one side for female *difuntas* and the other side for male *difuntos.* This arrangement corresponds to statements about distinctions between *angelito* and *difunto* but does not tell us about how they actually bury their dead. My own observation of burial attests to an entirely different arrangement than the ones stated by natives. It turns out burial is done on family grounds. Persons related to each other, constituting family, are buried near each other. I was faced with the same kind of nebulousness when I asked about the use of the "sacred stone." They use a stone for pounding grave earth during burial. But there are two stones, a small and a big one. Again there was disagreement and vagueness as to whether it is sex or marriage that determined the differential use of the stones.

Don't the natives know what they are doing? Sure, they do. They also convey important information when they show uncertainty as well as certainty about the meaning of a concept. When natives indicate that a concept is very well-defined this tells me something about the concept itself—that certain concepts are charcterized by certain properties. When they show uncertainty as to the ideological boundaries of a concept (as they did with cemetery) they are telling me that certain concepts are loosely defined in any system of concepts.

Let us go back to case 16, the Bruja Myth. Cemetery serves as a linking category between house and field, in the one sense linking two boundary points within the spatial universe, and in the other linking the human world with the superhuman world.

Furthermore, we have seen how the witch goes to the cemetery, transforms itself into a buzzard, goes to the field to do its evil, then goes back to the cemetery, retransforms itself into a person, and goes home. Cemetery, then, also serves as a transforming category.

The conceptual opposition of "house/field" is therefore related by a mediating category "cemetery," which in this particular conceptual environment mediates in the sense of "linking/transforming." There are other examples of concepts in the Zapotec culture that are clearly characterized in the same fashion. One interesting example which I recommend is the "Jesus/Devil" opposition mediated by "witch."[5]

PROPERTIES OF CONCEPTUAL CATEGORIES

According to my analysis of the Zapotec system I found that there are various sets of conceptual categories drawn from various cultural domains. Some of them are represented in matrix form shown below.

Looking at this Zapotec conceptual structure we find two kinds of categories—sets of categories in (1) binary opposition, such as power/nonpower, house/field, etc., related by (2) mediating categories.

Examining these categories I find that those in binary form are well-defined, rigidly marked, and inflexible in categorical boundary; and are associated with complex internal differentiation and strong affect. They are "closed" in boundary. I call these "closed concepts." Conversely, the relating categories are loosely defined, highly flexible, and "open" in boundary. I call these "open concepts." Closed conceptual categories are mediated by open conceptual categories.

Belief Systems Have To Have Both Closed and Open Concepts

Belief systems are constrained in two ways. There are constraints derived (1)

5. Fadwa El Guindi, "The Internal Structure of the Zapotec Conceptual System," *Journal of Symbolic Anthropology* 1(1973):26-31.

FIGURE 5.8
ZAPOTEC CONCEPTS AND DOMAINS

	Zapotec Conceptual Structure			Domains
Ritual Base	*Angelito*	*Difunto*	Marriage	Ritual
	House	Field	Cemetery	Spatial
	Jesus	Devil	Witch	Moral
	Power	Nonpower	Mediator	Sociological

from the properties of beliefs as a system; and constraints relating to (2) the capacity of the human mind to compute and process information.

For any dynamic system to function properly, it must have ways that would enable it to accommodate novel input. Static systems lack such accommodation. However, constant change takes place in human systems; there is constant input. The anthropologist entering a culture to live with and study a people is an example of novel input into the system of these people. The people have to do something about it. Either they will accommodate such novel input; that is, in the case of the anthropologist, they would accept her and categorize her, or they will reject her. If the system were completely closed and strongly defined, there would be no possibility for accommodation.

Like computer language, inputs have to be in certain forms. A novel input in an unaccommodating form will either be extruded or will destroy the system. Holmberg gives us the following example of extruded input:

Case 17: The Wells That Failed.

This case occurred in the village of Viru, located 300 miles north of Lima. The village is dependent for its water on a small river that drains neighboring Andean highlands. The river is adequate for irrigation for only six months out of the year. Because rainfall is so sparse in the area, the people cannot raise a second crop and often barely raise the single crop.

The village has been isolated from the rest of Peru for most of its history until 1939 when a paved road passing by the village was completed. Seasonal variations in the water supply and the control of such variation for the good of the community were explained through their conceptual system.

". . . such natural phenomena as the water were thought to be controlled by supernatural forces—as represented by images of the Catholic saints—which could be influenced only by the celebration of the feast days of certain saints. In Viru, for example, the first water of the new agricultural year generally appears in the irrigation ditch soon after the celebration of the fiesta of the Virgin of Sorrow, . . . on the twelfth of December. If the year is dry, it is believed that this fiesta has not been properly celebrated and that the Virgin is castigating the people. If the year continues to be dry, the image of St. Isidore, patron of farmers, may be taken out on a religious procession and worshipped at the river until water comes."[6]

In 1947 the government offered to solve the water shortage by drilling wells in the area. But from the beginning they had difficulties. Only a few people were willing to help widen roads and move the drilling equipment, even though no agricultural work was being done in this season. Laborers had to be hired at considerable expense, instead, and even then few were willing to work. In addition, the project technicians had trouble finding places to stay in the village or even families to cook lunches for them.

The opinion of the villagers about the project varied; some supported it, while others were doubtful of its success or seemed to know nothing about it. "Still others spoke openly against it, saying that it was all politics, that the geologists . . . did not know their business, . . . and that if water were struck the village would not benefit by it anyway."[7]

Almost no one had enough interest to visit the drilling site, only two miles away. Because of the poor cooperation and apparent lack of interest, the project engineer recommended that no further wells be drilled, and the one well that had been finished was not furnished with a

6. Allan R. Holmberg, "The Wells That Failed," in *Human Problems in Technological Change,* ed. E. H. Spicer (New York: Russell Sage Foundation, 1952), p. 119.

7. Ibid., p. 116.

pump or other necessary equipment. The reaction of most villagers was one of "I told you so!"[8]

Let us now look at an example of novel input that was forced onto a system in a form that could not be accommodated. Sharp describes the Yir Yiront case which shows how their system was destroyed because it could not accommodate the steel axe.

Case 18: There Is No Room For A Steel Axe in the Australian System.

The Yir Yiront are a group of Australian aborigines. Since their initial recorded contact with a Dutch expedition in 1623 they had only sporadic contacts with Europeans through the early part of the twentieth century. These were very unfortunate for the Yir Yiront because the whites killed them and kidnapped their children to use as slaves on their ranches. Finally their territory was set aside as a reserve and they were allowed to continue their traditional, stone-age way of life into the twentieth century.

In 1915 an Anglican mission began filtering a number of technological items to this group. One such item is the steel axe. Very rapidly the steel axe replaced the aboriginal stone axe because of its superior efficiency and durability. But their system was not ready for it. The stone axe was a very important element in Yir Yiront culture. Only men could make and own the axe. Stone for the heads was not available in their oceanside environment, and they relied on their neighbors 400 miles to the south to obtain it. That was done through an elaborate system of trading.

Every male had at least one permanent trading partner with whom he exchanged spears tipped with stingray spines for stone axe heads. These exchanges were accompanied by elaborate ritual activities.

The stone axe was used by men, women, and children in important tasks, such as food gathering, firewood collecting, building, and making tools and weapons. Men retained ownership of the axe, women and children were required to borrow it. Borrowing was highly institutionalized and was based on kinship behavior patterns. Axes can be borrowed from husband, elder brother, or father. It served to establish status and role relationships. Women and children were dependent on and subordinate to men, younger men were subordinate to older men, etc. Such borrowing, therefore, expressed and symbolized male superiority in their system.

As a result of introducing the steel axe in that system sex, age, and kinship roles became confused. Younger men, women and children could now own axes and therefore do not have to go through the channels of borrowing and lending. Another outcome was the weakening of traditional trading partnerships and the decline of the ritual that went with it. There was also a loss of leadership patterns that were clearly defined before.

In terms of Yir Yiront beliefs, every aspect of their culture was accompanied by a myth that justified its existence and gave it meaning. Their system was totemic. Every element in their culture was associated with a class of people. Every object was identified with a kin group. One clan had more than a hundred objects identified with it. Two important clans are Head-to-the-East Corpse, which is associated with the color white as well as with death, and Sunlit Cloud Iguana, which is associated with the stone axe. The steel axe was paradoxical for their totemic system. Because it is steel, obviously introduced by white man who is both white and lethal, it became identified with Head-to-the-East Corpse. But being an axe, it remained associated with Sunlit Cloud Iguana. There was overlapping, confusion, and uncertainty in terms of how such a foreign "concept" fits their existing conceptual system as symbolized in their totemic classification. Although the steel axe replaced the stone axe physically, it was unable to replace it conceptually. Stone axe is a well-defined, rigidly bounded, closed

8. Ibid., pp. 113-123.

concept. As Sharp puts it: "the most disturbing effects of the steel axe . . . developed in the realm of traditional ideas, sentiments and values. These were undermined at a rapidly mounting rate, without new conceptions being defined to replace them. The result was a mental and moral void which foreshadowed the collapse and destruction of all Yir Yiront culture, if not, indeed, the extinction of the biological group itself."[9]

But anthropology is full of examples of change. Cultural systems are constantly dealing with accommodating change, that is, novel input in a form that can be accommodated within the system. Let us go once more to the Zapotec to see how anthropologists can be incorporated in cultures.

Case 19: There Is Room for an Anthropologist in the Zapotec Ritual System.

The Zapotec people in the community I studied were getting used to my presence. I had attended every ritual that took place during my stay, particularly every death ritual. This was one more death ritual, a *difunta* (female married dead).

On the ninth day after a *difunto* ritual begins there is the ritual of *levantar la cruz* (raising the cross). Special categories of people are invited to attend and are obligated to perform certain services. There are kin present, and there are the ritual officials who attend to perform such functions as prayer and burial. The major event of that particular ritual is raising the cross, which is supervised by ritual officials but has to be mainly performed by a fictive kin who is the same sex as the deceased, in this case, a *comadre* (a female coparent).

The ritual seemed to roll along smoothly. Slowly as the time for raising the cross approached I noticed much confusion and whispering. Twenty minutes later the *casera* (the woman of the house) came toward me and very formally asked if I would raise the cross. I was flattered. But I was also very confused. They did not give me any reason, and I was fully aware of the rigid sociological categorization in ritual. Boundaries are not casually crossed. I was not a comadre to the deceased. I had to know, and like any persistent anthropologist, I asked. I was told that the only female relatives who were present at the moment in that ritual were *cunadas* (in-laws). Only a *comadre* can raise the cross to a female deceased. In other words, it is someone of the category "fictive" who should raise the cross. Only category "affines" were present.

But why me? Of course I was already in the house where the ritual is taking place, and I was already accepted in their culture. But in order to be in ritual one has to be categorized. Supposing they needed category affine (inlaw) or category "consanguine" (blood relative), would they have chosen me? My hypothesis would be no. According to my analysis, affine and consanguine are closed categories, but fictive is open. It was fictive that required personnel.

What would have happened if that category did not need personnel? Would they let me stay "loose" and uncategorized? No, no loose people are allowed in ritual. In all the earlier death rituals I attended I was categorized "ritual official," another open category. I was always asked to eat with the ritual officials at meal time. I did not know why then. But categories eat separately.

Therefore to accommodate novel input belief system must have open aspects. In Reitman's terms:

"It is easy to suggest why so much of human activity involved open, ill-defined statements. The brain stores and has the ability to utilize large amounts of information. With respect to that stored information, detailed new information often would be redundant. Open state-

9. Lauriston Sharp, "Steel Axes for Stone Age Australians," in *Human Problems in Technological Change,* pp. 69-90.

ments enable us to avoid that redundancy in perceiving, communicating, and thinking. It is inefficient for an intelligent system communicating with others or with itself over time to specify objects and ideas fully if their properties were readily filled in or inferred as needed from information already available. Similarly, why specify a new object or detail if it can be indicated simply by naming some already stored schema together with properties of modifications peculiar to the new instance."[10]

But systems cannot be completely open and adaptable because of the information-processing limitation of the mind.[11] If every culture bearer had to work with open concepts, then he would be constantly dealing with problems of decidability. He would never know (in a formal sense) whether a solution method existed for the encoding and decoding of the environment, simply because there would be so much uncertainty involved in the operation of open systems.

In sum: open categories are necessary for the encoding of novel input, closed categories are necessary for the system to be manipulable by the limited computing machinery of the human mind.

CONCLUSION

I believe that there is strong indication that humans conceptualize the world and their experiences in it in some systematic way, i.e., in the form of a system. They use that system as a generalized model to guide their activities and to understand concrete social situations.

Insisting that religion, as Tylor told us, is a "belief in spiritual beings" or looking for Durkheimian special moods of "sacredness" that demarcates the religious from the secular, will leave us where they have left us. We cannot deny the value of their distinctions. They are good but not enough. Anthropology has to keep moving forward.

I tried to make sense of what the Zapotec "know" which led them to have *me* raise the cross. Though a model of natives' knowledge of their culture is abstract, it can serve in understanding what the natives say and what they do.

They "know" something at "some level" that led them to give María, an 87-year-old woman, an *angelito* funeral when she died. I had thought about her when I was considering hypothetical cases to confirm the assumptions made in my proposed conceptual model. There was María, an old woman who had never married. My informant laughed when I told him that following my analysis of their system she would die an *angelito*. He thought it would be ridiculous. But it was not ridiculous. I received a letter from him that María had died. Indeed, they gave her a happy ritual. In her 87th year she died as *angelito*, the ritual that the natives tell us is given for children.

For Further Reading

Rossi, Ino, ed. *The Unconscious in Culture*. New York: E. P. Dutton & Co., 1974. A collection of articles on the theory of structuralism, which shows the development of an independent school of theory going beyond Lévi-Strauss's seminal works. Documents the debates over some of the key issues in structuralist theory.

Bibliography

El Guindi, Fadwa. 1973. "The Internal Structure of the Zapotec Conceptual System." *Journal of Symbolic Anthropology* 1:16-34.

———. "The Structural Correlates of Power in

10. Walter Reitman, "The Uses of Experience: Open Statements, Ill-Defined Strategies, and Intelligent Information Processing," in *Cognitive Studies*, ed. J. Hellmuth (New York: Brunner, Nazel, 1970), p. 211.

11. G. A. Miller, "The Magical Number Seven, Plus or Minus Two: Some Limits on Our Capacity for Processing Information," *Psychological Review* 63 (1965): 81-97.

Ritual." In *Anthropology of Power*. Edited by N. R. Adams and R. Fogelson. New York: Academic Press, in press.

———. "Internal Constraints on Structure." In *New Trends in Structural Anthropology*. Edited by Ino Rossi (forthcoming).

———. "Structure and Natives' Knowledge of Culture." In *Toward the Sociology of Symbolic Structures. Edited by Ino Rossi* (forthcoming).

Holmberg, Allan R. 1952. "The Wells that Failed." In *Human Problems in Technological Change*. Edited by E. H. Spicer. New York: Russell Sage Foundation.

Miller, G. A. 1965. "The Magical Number Seven, Plus or Minus Two: Some Units on Our Capacity for Processing Information." *Psychological Review* 63:81-97.

Reitman, Walter. 1970. "The Uses of Experience: Open Statements, Ill-defined Strategies, and Intelligent Information Processing." In *Cognitive Studies*. Edited by J. Hellmuth. New York: Brunner, Nazel.

Sharp, Lauriston. 1952. "Steel Axes for Stone Age Australians." In *Human Problems in Technological Change*. Edited by E. H. Spicer. New York: Russell Sage Foundation.

Glossary

Affinal—Related by marriage.

Aguardiente—Rumlike liquor from sugar cane that got replaced by mescal (which is made from the maguey plant) in many areas of rural Oaxaca.

Anthropomorphous Beings—Superhuman beings thought to have the attributes of humans.

Autochthonous—Stemming from the earth or ground; by extension, native to a particular territory.

Cargo Cult—One of a series of religious movements in New Guinea triggered by the initial contact with Westerners. The arrival of the Europeans was seen as the end of the mundane world with all its normal values, hardships and duties and the beginning of an era of abundant material goods (cargo) and a utopian existence.

Causal Relationship—A relationship whereby one phenomenon causes another and hence precedes it in time.

Collective Representations—Objects or acts which symbolize for a people the crucial elements of their conceptual system and the links or operations that relate these elements. They are collective because they are defined or performed by a group of individuals, and are representations because they bring abstract ideas into the real world.

Comadre—Reciprocal term (Spanish) referring to a fictive kinship relationship between a godmother and the parents of her godchild.

Comparative Study—The kind of study that looks for the explanation of a custom or other social phenomenon by examining it in two or more unrelated societies. This is done to rule out explanations which depend on purely local factors.

Consanguine—A blood relative.

Consuegro—Reciprocal term (Spanish) referring to the affinal relationship between two fathers whose offspring are married to each other.

Cultural Relativism—Judging other ways of life in terms of their own standards as opposed to absolute standards. According to this notion no culture is better than any other culture.

Culture—An ideational system, a system of knowledge. By culture I mean the ideas, meanings, and knowledge—conscious and unconscious—that people share.

Culture Specific—Phenomena associated with a specific way of life.

Cuñada—Sister-in-law (Spanish).

Dialectical Relationship—The logical relationship between two phenomena that are complete opposites. This involves a synthesis of oppositions through mediators. Unlike *causal* relationships, dialectical relations are *not* constrained by (a) lineal direction, as in the statement, "Earthquake cause destruction, but destruction does not cause earthquakes"; nor by (b) chronological sequence, as in "Lightning occurs before thunder, therefore lightning must cause thunder."

Empirical—Pertaining to concrete data as opposed to abstract theorizing.

Establishing Rapport—The process by which anthropologists in the field work toward being accepted by the people who are being studied.

Ethnocentrism—Judging other ways of life by the standards of one's own culture.

Excision—Surgical removal of the clitoris and at times the external labia. This operation is carried out in Nubia and other non-Western societies as part of a girl's rite of passage from childhood to womanhood.

Fictive—A relative by a social tie. Fictive relationships are modeled on blood relations, such as godparenthood.

Ghost Dance—A religious movement that sprang up among the Native Americans west of the Mississippi between 1870 and 1890; it predicted the return of the dead and the old order of life with its prosperity; at the same time the encroaching European settlers would be destroyed.

Guelaguetza—Refers to an institutionalized form of lending and borrowing of items in specified quantities; it tends to be activated more during fiestas and rituals and exists in Oaxaca, Mexico.

Homology—A relationship of logical correspondence or similarity.

Kinship—The network of relationships created by (a) genealogical connections, thus consanguineal kinship; (b) social ties modeled on the natural relations of genealogical parenthood, thus fictive kinship; and (c) alliances through marriage, thus affinal kinship. Kinship relations are universal, and are *bilateral* in that they include both the mother and the father. They form systems with a definite starting point, ego, and with positions that are defined relative to each other.

Kula Ring—The Trobriand Islands of the western Pacific are united into a big ring of ceremonial exchange. They exchange two ceremonial objects: long necklaces of shell disks move clockwise around the island ring; white armshells travel counterclockwise.

Liminality—Transitional stage between two phases in ritual, used by van Gennep and Turner.

Mettoki—Nubian dialect spoken by the Kenuz Nubians of Egypt.

Misterio—Mystery, secret (Spanish).

Mytheme—A term coined by Lévi-Strauss to refer to the smallest meaningful constituent unit in a myth that includes bundles of relations.

Paleolithic—Belonging to the period between 10,000 to 60,000 years ago.

Phoneme—Abstract unit of sound that exists on the phonemic level. Trubetzkoy conceived of it as consisting of bundles of distinctive features.

Phonemic—Refers to only those sounds or their abstract representations that signal meaning differences—that is, that tell us that one word means something different from another.

Phonetic—Refers to features that physically distinguish one speech sound from another.

Propitiation—A ritual offering made to gain the favor or forgiveness of one or more deities.

Subculture—A group of people within a particular society who identify and at some time associate with each other and have in common a set of ideas or meanings, an elaborated subset of the larger cultural system. These ideas are harmonious with the wider cultural system but provide more specific information about domains not characterized in detail by the wider culture. For example, all members of American culture can recognize a gunshot, but those with military training will "hit the dirt" when they hear one close by.

Universals—Phenomena which are found all over the world without exception.

Viguela—Mexican musical instrument that has been replaced by the guitar in the Zapotec culture.

Index

Abstract level, 23, 39, 56, 63
Affinal kinship, 52, 62, 65
All Saints Festival, 8, 9, 20, 56
American Indians, 20, 27-29
Americans
  conceptual system of, 1-3, 10, 11, 19, 20, 43
  values of, 1-3, 10, 11
Andaman Islanders, 45
Animatism, 9, 17
Animism, 8, 9, 17
Arabs, 3, 7, 34, 36
'asabiyya, 7
Autochthony
  in Oedipus myth, 38
  in Trobriand myth, 14, 19
Axes, steel and stone, 15, 61-62
Azande, 12, 18

Bascom, William, 29
Belief systems, 1, 3, 18, 46, 59
Binary codes, 22, 34, 35, 50, 55, 58, 59
Blackfoot, 27
Boas, Franz, 25
Boundaries
  of the acceptable, 2, 3
  of conceptual categories, 1, 3, 23, 57, 58, 59
  of the universe, 1, 3, 57, 58
Buddhism, 10
Bushmen, 26

Cargo cults, 20, 65
Categorizing new phenomena, 1, 3, 60, 61, 62
Causal relationships, 1, 14, 65
Ceremony, definition of, 39
Chomsky, Noam, 35
Christianity, beliefs of, 1, 5, 6
Civilization, 6, 7
Classification of the universe
  by natives, 43-44, 58, 59
  related to conceptual system, 43-44, 59
Closed conceptual categories, 59, 60, 61, 62, 63
Community, 12
Comparative studies of religion, 17
Conceptual systems, 1, 19, 20, 21, 61, 63
Concrete level, 21-22, 39, 51, 63
Consanguineal kinship, 52, 62, 65
Content, as opposed to structure, 34, 36, 39, 51
Cultural relativism, 10, 17, 20, 65
Culture, 1, 3, 7, 11, 32, 33, 34, 65

Death
  among the Zapotec, 8, 9, 49-56, 58, 62
  religious theories of, 8
Dialectical relationships, 7, 66
Distinctive features (linguistics), 35
Dogma, 1
Dreams, religious interpretations of, 8
Durkheim, Émile, 9-12, 20, 43, 45, 63

Egypt, 1, 2, 3, 10, 14, 15, 20, 32, 33, 49
Empiricism, 5, 6, 7, 66
Eskimo, 26
Ethnocentrism, 5, 6, 13, 66
Ethnoscience, 43-44
Evil eye, as an explanatory device, 14-15
Evolutionism, 5, 6, 7, 11, 13, 17

Fictive kinship, 3, 22, 52, 62, 66
Frake, Charles O., 44
Frazer, Sir James, 12-13, 15
Functionalism, 26

Geertz, Clifford, 19, 21
Ghost dance movement, 20, 66

INDEX
Continued

Gluckman, Max, 39
Guelaguetza exchange network, 52, 66

Hako (Plains Indian ritual), 29
Halle, Morris, 35
Harrison, Jane, 25
Hidatsa, 27
Hocart, A.M., 25
Holmberg, Allan, 60
Homans, George, 45
Hooke, S. H., 26
Human mind
- limitations of, 34, 35, 60, 63
- universal properties of, 15, 25, 34, 44, 45

Ibn Khaldun, 6-8, 11
Ideologies, 1
Information
- as conveyed by society, 21, 34
- its processing by the human mind, 34, 35, 60, 62, 63
- and myth, 21, 34
- and ritual, 21
- verbal and non-verbal, 21, 46

Islam, 5, 6, 7

Jakobson, Roman, 35
Judaism, 1, 2, 5, 7

Keesing, Roger, viii, 21, 44, 46
Kinship and kinshipping, 3, 29, 51, 52, 66
Kluckhohn, Clyde, 19-20, 26
Kula exchange system, 13, 66
Kwakiutl mythology, 38

Lang, Andrew, 25
Law of contagion (Frazer), 12-13
Law of similarity (Frazer), 12-13
Law of sympathy (Frazer), 12-13
Leach, Edmund, 21, 46
Legend, 29, 30
Lessa, William, vii, 33
Lévi-Strauss, Claude, vii, viii, 10, 15, 23, 26-29, 33-39, 44, 46, 49
Lévy-Bruhl, Lucien, 13
Linguistics, 34, 35, 36, 44

Magic
- contagious, 12-13
- homeopathic, 12-13
- opposed to religion, 12, 17
- related to myth, 14
- related to science, 12, 13, 14, 15
- sympathetic, 12, 13

Malinowski, Bronislaw, 12-15, 17, 19, 32, 45, 49
Mana (Polynesian concept), 9, 12
Mandan (Native American people), 27, 28, 29
Marett, Robert R., 9, 10
Marriage, among the Zapotec, 22-23, 50-51, 52, 54, 55, 56
Matlazigua (Zapotec), 30, 31, 32, 58
Mauss, Marcel, 43
Mediators (in conceptual systems), 22, 52, 55, 56, 59
Mentalistic approach, 7, 18
Mohave, 26
Monotheism, 7
Moslems, beliefs of, 1, 2, 3, 7, 20
Multivocality of symbols (Turner), 41
Mushahra (Nubia), 14, 15
Myth
- anthropological theories of, 25, 26, 29, 31
- and belief, 38, 46
- as charter, 19, 31, 32, 33
- as culture-reflector, 19, 31, 32, 33
- definitions of, 29, 30
- functions, 19, 32
- as a logical model, 33, 34
- and ritual, 25, 26, 27, 28, 29, 30, 32
- as seen by psychoanalysis, 25

Mytheme, 36, 66

Ndembu (Zambia), 40, 41, 42, 43, 45
New Guinea, 20
Nubia, 10, 14, 15, 18, 20, 32, 33, 34, 49

Oedipus myth, 36-38
Open conceptual categories, 59, 62, 63
Oppositions
- in language, 35
- in Ndenbu ritual, 41, 42
- in Pawnee myth, 27-29, 36
- in Zapotec conceptual system, 22, 50, 51, 52, 55, 56, 58, 59

Origin myths, 19, 25, 27, 32

Paleolithic man, 5, 66
Pawnee, 27-29, 36
Peru, 60
Phonemic, 35, 66, 67
Phonetic, 36, 67
Phonology, 35
Prague school of linguistics, 35
Primitive thought, 8, 9, 10, 12, 13, 15, 25
Profane (as opposed to sacred), 10, 11, 39, 63
Psychological approach to religion, 18, 19, 20, 46
Pueblo mythology, 38

Radcliffe-Brown, A. R., 20, 45
Raglan, Lord, 26

Rapport, R., 2, 3, 66
Rationality, 13, 18, 32
Reitman, Walter, 62-63
Religion
  anthropological view of, vii, 5, 6, 7, 10
  definitions of, 1, 3, 8, 9, 10, 11, 12, 63
  development of, 6, 7, 11, 13
  and the emotions, 11, 21
  as an explanation of the mysterious, 8, 10, 18
  hypothetical beginnings of, 6, 8, 10, 17
  as integrating customs and beliefs into a system, 3, 9-10, 11, 12, 18, 20, 21
  as a means of social integration, 3, 11, 12, 20, 21
  philosophical treatment of, 5, 6
  psychological functions of, 19, 20
  relationship to society of, 6, 7, 12
  as a social phenomenon, 7, 11, 20
  as a source of social institutions, 11
  validating functions of, 18, 19
Rites of passage, 40
Ritual
  as associated with social transition, 39, 40, 41
  and collective sentiment, 45
  definition of, 39
  in relation to the emotions, 11, 45
  as a means of defining concepts, 21, 23
  as a means of encoding information, 21, 34, 46
  as a means of reducing anxiety, 45
  as a means of social integration, 20, 21, 22, 23
  a part of all religions, 8, 9-10, 12, 25, 46
  redundancy of, 21
  relation to myth, 10, 25, 26, 27, 28, 29, 30
  as symbolic organization, 41
Ritual base, 56, 59
Roles, 2
Romans, 26
Rules and rule violation, 2, 11, 19, 39

Sacred (as opposed to profane), 9, 10, 11, 30, 39, 63
Sacred symbols, 10, 19, 20, 32-33
Saints' days, 20
Sanctions, 2, 19
Savage, as viewed by the Victorians, 6
Science, 6, 7, 8,
  as related to magic, 12, 13, 14, 15
Shamanism, 27, 28
Sharp, Lavriston, 61-62
Social solidarity, 7, 11, 21
Society, 7, 10, 11, 12
"Soul," as an explanatory device, 8, 18
Spatial categories
  in Turner's analysis, 41-43
  in Zapotec myth, 56, 57, 58, 59
Spiro, Milford, 18
Structural analysis, 33, 34, 36, 49
Structural anthropology, 33, 34, 38, 39, 44
Structure
  in language, myth, ritual, 33-38, 39, 51
  as opposed to content, 36, 39, 51
  and Zapotec ritual, 38, 49, 51, 52, 54, 55, 56
Symbols, 10, 11, 19, 21, 25, 38, 40, 41, 42, 43, 45

Taxonomic approaches
  to myth, 29-30, 31
  to oral tradition, 29-30, 31
  to religion, 14, 17
  to ritual, 39
Toda, 26
Totemism, 17, 39, 61
Trobriand Islanders, 13, 18, 19, 32
Trubetzkoy, Nicolaii, 34, 35, 36
Tuareg (North Africa), 34
Turner, Victor, vii, 39, 40, 41, 42, 43, 44-45
Tylor, Edward B. 8, 10, 17, 63

Unconscious
  information, 21, 23
  structure, 34, 36, 39
Universals, 17, 25, 34, 40, 41, 44, 67

van Gennep, Arnold, 40

Witchcraft
  among the Azande, 18
  among the Zapotec, 56, 57, 58, 59
World religions, 5

Yir Yoront (Australians), 61, 62

Zapotec
  conceptual system of, 2, 8-9, 14, 21-23, 34, 50, 51, 52, 54, 55, 56, 58, 59, 62, 63
  myths of, 8, 21, 30, 31, 56, 57, 58, 59
  ritual, 9, 21, 22, 38, 49, 50, 51, 52, 53, 54, 55, 56, 62, 63